THE MEDIEVAL LIBRARY UNDER
THE GENERAL EDITORSHIP OF
SIR ISRAEL GOLLANCZ, Litt.D., F.B.A.

# Cligés

## A Romance

Translated by

### L. J. Gardiner, M.A.

from

the Old French of

### Chrétien de Troyes

With a Frontispiece

*A Twelfth Century Knight in full armour*

# CLIGÉS : A ROMANCE NOW TRANSLATED BY L. J. GARDINER, M.A. : FROM THE OLD FRENCH OF CHRÉTIEN DE TROYES

COOPER SQUARE PUBLISHERS, INC.
NEW YORK
1966

Published 1966 by Cooper Square Publishers, Inc.
59 Fourth Avenue, New York, N. Y. 10003
Library of Congress Catalog Card No. 66-23315

Printed in the United States of America
by Noble Offset Printers, Inc., New York, N. Y. 10003

# INTRODUCTION

It is six hundred and fifty years since Chrétien de Troyes wrote his *Cligés*. And yet he is wonderfully near us, whereas he is separated by a great gulf from the rude trouvères of the Chansons de Gestes and from the Anglo-Saxon Chronicle, which was still dragging out its weary length in his early days. Chrétien is as refined, as civilised, as composite as we are ourselves; his ladies are as full of whims, impulses, sudden reserves, self-debate as M. Paul Bourget's heroines; while the problems of conscience and of emotion which confront them are as complex as those presented on the modern stage. Indeed, there is no break between the Breton romance and the psychological-analytical novel of our own day.

Whence comes this amazing modernity and complexity? From many sources:—Provençal love-lore,

Oriental subtlety, and Celtic mysticism—all blended by that marvellous dexterity, style, *malice*, and *mesure* which are so utterly French that English has no adequate words for them. We said "Celtic mysticism," but there is something else about Chrétien which is also Celtic, though very far from being "mystic." We talk a great deal nowadays about Celtic melancholy, Celtic dreaminess, Celtic "other-worldliness"; and we forget the qualities that made Cæsar's Gauls, St. Paul's Galatians, so different from the grave and steadfast Romans,—that *fond gaulois* that has made the Parisian the typical Frenchman. A different being, this modern Athenian, from the mystic Irish peasant we see in the poetic modern Irish drama!—and yet both are Celts.

Not much "other-worldliness" about Chrétien! He is as *positif* as any man can be. His is not the world of Saint Louis, of the Crusaders, of the Cathedral-builders. In *Cligés* there is no religious atmosphere at all. We hear scarcely anything of Mass, of bishops, of convents. When he mentions *Tierce* or *Prime*, it is merely to tell us the hour at which something happened —and this something is never a religious service. There is nothing behind the glamour of arms and love, except for the *cas de conscience* presented by the lovers. Nothing but names and framework are Celtic; the spirit, with its refinements and its hair-splitting, is Provençal. But what a brilliant whole! what art! what *mesure !* Our thoughts turn to the gifted women of the age,—as subtle, as interesting, and as unscrupulous as the women of the Renaissance—to Eleanor of Aquitaine, a reigning princess, a troubadour, a Crusader, the wife of two kings, the mother of two kings, to the last intriguing and pulling the strings of political power—

  "An Ate, stirring him [King John] to blood and strife."

The twelfth century was an age in which women had full scope—in which the Empress Maud herself took the field against her foe, in which Stephen's queen seized a fortress, in which a wife could move her husband to war or to peace, in which a Marie of Champagne (Eleanor's daughter) could set the tone to great poets and choose their subjects.

If, then, this woman-worship, this complexity of love, this self-debating, first comes into literature with

Chrétien de Troyes, and is still with us, no more interesting work exists than his earliest masterpiece, *Cligés*. The delicate and reticent Soredamors; the courteous and lovable Guinevere; the proud and passionate Fenice, who will not sacrifice her fair fame and chastity; the sorceress Thessala, ancestress of Juliet's nurse;—these form a gallery of portraits unprecedented in literature.

The translator takes this opportunity of thanking Mr. B. J. Hayes, M.A., of St. John's College, Cambridge, for occasional help, and also for kindly reading the proofs.

# CLIGÉS

THE clerk who wrote the tale of Erec and Enid and translated the Commandments of Ovid and the Art of Love, and composed the Bite of the Shoulder, and sang of King Mark and of the blonde Iseult, and of the metamorphosis of the Hoopoe and of the Swallow and of the Nightingale, is now beginning a new tale of a youth who was in Greece of the lineage of King Arthur. But before I tell you anything of him, you shall hear his father's life—whence he was and of what lineage. So valiant was he and of such proud spirit, that to win worth and praise he went from Greece to England, which was then called Britain. We find this story, that I desire to tell and to relate to you, recorded in one of the books of the library of my lord Saint Peter at Beauvais. Thence was taken the tale from which Chrétien framed this romance. The book, which truthfully bears witness to the story, is very ancient; for this reason it is all the more to be believed. From the books which we possess, we know the deeds of the ancients and of the world which aforetime was. This our books have taught us : that Greece had the first renown in chivalry and in learning. Then came chivalry to Rome, and the heyday of learning, which now is come into France. God grant that she be maintained there, and that her home there please her so much that never may depart from France the honour which has there taken up its abode. God had lent that glory to others, but no man talks any longer either more or less about Greeks and Romans ; talk of them has ceased, and the bright glow is extinct.

Chrétien begins his tale—as the story relates to us —which tells of an emperor, mighty in wealth and honour, who ruled Greece and Constantinople. There was a very noble empress, by whom the emperor had two children. But the first was of such an age before the other was born that, if he had willed, he might have become a knight and held all the empire. The first was named Alexander, the younger was called Alis. The father, too, had for name Alexander, and the mother had for name Tantalis. I will straightway leave speaking of the empress Tantalis, of the emperor, and of Alis. I will speak to you of Alexander, who was so great-hearted and proud that he

did not stoop to become a knight in his own realm.
He had heard mention made of King Arthur, who was
reigning at that time, and of the barons which he ever
maintained in his retinue, wherefore his Court was
feared and famed throughout the world. Howe'er the
end may fall out for him, and whate'er may come of it
for the lad, there is nought that will hold him from his
yearning to go to Britain; but it is meet that he take
leave of his father before he goes to Britain or to
Cornwall. Alexander the fair, the valiant, goes to
speak to the emperor in order to ask permission and
to take his leave. Now will he tell him what is his
vow, and what he would fain do and take in hand.
" Fair sire, that I may be schooled in honour and win
worth and renown, a boon," quoth he, " I venture to
crave of you—a boon that I would have you give me;
never defer it now for me if you are destined to grant
it." The emperor had no thought of being vexed
for that, either much or little; he is bound to desire
and to covet honour for his son above aught else.
He would deem himself to be acting well—would
deem? ay, and he would be so acting—if he increased
his son's honour. " Fair son," quoth he, " I grant
you your good pleasure, and tell me what you would
have me give you." Now the lad has done his work
well, and right glad was he of it, when is granted him

the boon that he so longed to have. " Sire," quoth
he, " would you know what you have promised me ?
I wish to have, in great store, of your gold and of your
silver, and comrades from your retinue, such as I
shall will to choose ; for I wish to go forth from your
empire, and I shall go to offer my service to the king
who reigns over Britain, that he may dub me knight.
Never, indeed, on any day as long as I live shall I
wear visor on my face or helm on my head, I warrant
you, till King Arthur gird on my sword, if he deign
to do it ; for I will receive arms of no other." The
emperor, without more ado, replies : " Fair son, in
God's name say not so. This land and mighty
Constantinople are wholly yours. You must not
hold me a niggard, when I would fain give you
so fair a boon. Soon will I have you crowned,
and a knight shall you be to-morrow. All Greece
shall be in your hand, and you shall receive from
your barons—as indeed you ought to receive—their
oaths and homage. He who refuses this is no wise
man."

The lad hears the promise—namely, that his father
will dub him knight on the morrow after mass—but
says that he will prove himself coward or hero in
another land than his own. " If you will grant my
boon in that matter in which I have asked you, then

give me fur both grey and of divers colour, and good
steeds and silken attire; for before I am knight I will
fain serve King Arthur. Not yet have I so great
valour that I can bear arms. None by entreaty or by
fair words could persuade me not to go into the foreign
land to see the king and his barons, whose renown for
courtesy and for prowess is so great. Many high men
through their idleness lose great praise that they might
have if they wandered o'er the world. Repose and
praise agree ill together, as it seems to me; for a man
of might who is ever resting in no wise becomes
famous. Prowess is a burden to a cowardly man, and
cowardice is a burden to the brave; thus the twain
are diverse and contrary. And that man is a slave
to his possessions who is ever heaping them up and in-
creasing them. Fair sire, as long as I am allowed to
win renown, if I can avail so much, I will give my
pains and diligence to it."

At this, without doubt, the emperor feels joy and
anxiety—joy has he for that he perceives that his son
aims at valiant deeds, and anxiety on the other
hand, for that he is leaving him. But because of the
promise that he has made him, it behoves him to grant
his boon, whatever anxiety he feel about it; for an
emperor must not lie. "Fair son," quoth he, "I
ought not to fail to do your pleasure, since I see that

you aspire to honour. You may take from my trea-
sury two barques full of gold and silver; but take
care that you be very generous and courteous and
well-bred." Now is the youth right glad, for his
father promises him so much that he puts his treasure
at his free disposal, and exhorts and commands him
to give and to spend liberally; and also he tells him
the reason wherefore: "Fair son," quoth he, "be-
lieve me in this, that open-handedness is the lady and
queen who illumines all virtues, and it is not a whit
difficult to prove this. In what place could one find
a man, however mighty and magnificent he be, that
is not blamed if he be a niggard; or any man, how-
ever ill-reputed he be, whom liberality does not render
praised? Liberality of itself makes a man of honour
—which neither high rank, nor courtesy, nor know-
ledge, nor noble birth, nor wealth, nor strength, nor
chivalry, nor courage, nor lordship, nor beauty, nor
any other thing can do. But just as the rose is fairer
than any other flower when she buddeth fresh and
new, so where Liberality comes she holds herself
above all virtues, and she multiplies five hundredfold
the virtues that she finds in an honourable man who
proves his worth. There is so much to say about
liberality, that I could not tell the half of it." Well
has the lad succeeded in whatsoever he has requested

and asked, for his father has found for him all that his desire conceived. Exceeding sorrowful was the empress when she heard of the road which her son must needs follow; but whoever has grief and anxiety thereof, or whoever deems his conduct but folly, or blames and dissuades him, the youth, as quickly as he could, bade his ships be got ready; for he has no wish to stay longer in his own country. The ships were loaded that night by his command with wine, with meat, and with biscuits.

The ships are loaded in the harbour, and on the morrow with great joyaunce came Alexander to the sandy shore, and with him his comrades, who were fain of the journey. The emperor convoys him, and the empress, who was sad at heart. In the harbour they find the mariners in the ships beside the cliff. The sea was peaceful and smooth, the wind gentle, and the air serene. Alexander first of all, when he had parted from his father, on taking leave of the empress, whose heart was sad within her, enters from the boat into the ship, and his comrades with him. Four, three, and two they simultaneously strive to enter without delay. Full soon was the sail spread and the anchor of the barque weighed. Those on land, who were sore at heart for the lads whom they see departing, follow them with their

eyes' ken as far as they can; and so that they may
watch them the better and the further, they go
off and climb together a high peak by the shore.
Thence they watch their sorrow as far as they can
see them. They gaze at their own sorrow in sooth,
for great is their sorrow for the lads: may God
lead them to port without disaster and without
peril!

They were at sea all April and part of May. With-
out great peril and without alarm they made land
above Southampton. One day 'twixt Nones and
Vespers they cast anchor and have made the port.
The youths, who had never previously learned to
suffer discomfort or pain, had stayed on the sea, which
was not wholesome for them, so long that all are
pale, and all the strongest and most healthy are
weakened and nerveless. And nevertheless they show
great joy, for that they have escaped from the sea
and come hither where they would be. And because
they were suffering greatly, they lie that night above
Southampton, and show great joy, and let ask and
inquire whether the king is in England. They are
told that he is at Winchester, and that they can be
there full soon if they will depart with morning,
provided that they keep to the right way. This
news pleases them well; and on the morrow, when

the day is born, the lads wake up with morning, and
equip and prepare themselves. And when they were
equipped they have turned from above Southampton,
and have kept to the right way till they have reached
Winchester, where the king was tarrying. Before
Prime the Greeks had come to Court. They dis-
mount at the foot of the steps ; the squires and the
horses stayed in the court below, and the youths
ascend to the presence of the best king that ever was
or ever may be in the world. And when the king
sees them come, they please and delight him much ;
but ere they had come before him, they throw off
the cloaks from their necks, that they might not
be taken for clowns. Thus all having thrown off
their cloaks have come before the king. And the
barons one and all keep silence, for the youths please
them mightily, for that they see them fair and
comely. Never do they dream that they are all sons
of counts or of a king; yet truly so they were, and
they were in the flower of their youth, comely and
well set up in body ; and the robes that they wore
were of one cloth and one cut, of one appearance
and one colour. Twelve were they without their
lord, of whom I will tell you this much without more
ado, that none was better than he ; but without
arrogance and yet unabashed he stood with his

mantle off before the king, and was very fair and well shaped. He has kneeled down before him, and all the others, from courtesy, kneel beside their lord.

Alexander, whose tongue was sharpened to speak well and wisely, greets the king. "King," quoth he, "if renown lie not concerning you, since God made the first man, no king with faith in God was born so powerful as you. King, the report that is in men's mouths has brought me to your Court to serve and honour you; and if my service is pleasing, I will stay till I be a new-made knight at your hand, not at that of another. For never shall I be dubbed knight if I be not so by you. If my service so please you that you will to make me a knight, keep me, gracious king, and my comrades who are here." Straightway the king replies: "Friend," quoth he, "I reject not a whit either you or your company, but ye are all right welcome, for ye have the air, I well think it, of being sons of men of high rank. Whence are ye?" "We are from Greece." "From Greece?" "Truly are we." "Who is thy father?" "Faith, sire, the emperor." "And what is thy name, fair friend?" "Alexander was the name given me when I received salt and chrism, and Christianity and baptism." "Alexander, fair dear friend, I keep you right willingly, and much does it please

and joy me ; for you have done me exceeding great
honour in that you are come to my Court. It is my
good pleasure that you be honoured here as a noble
warrior and wise and gentle. Too long have you been
on your knees : rise, I bid you, and henceforth be
free of my Court and of me, for you have arrived
at a good haven."

Forthwith the Greeks rise. Blithe are they for that
the king has thus courteously kept them. Alexander is
welcome, for there is no lack of aught that he wishes,
nor is there any baron in the Court so high that he
does not speak him fair and welcome him. For he
is not foolish nor boastful, nor doth he vaunt his
noble birth. He makes himself known to Sir Gawain
and to the others, one by one. He makes himself much
loved by each ; even Sir Gawain loves him so much
that he hails him as friend and comrade. The Greeks
had taken in the town, at the house of a citizen, the
best lodging that they could find. Alexander had
brought great possessions from Constantinople : he
will desire above aught else to follow diligently the
emperor's advice and counsel—namely, that he should
have his heart wide-awake to give and to spend liber-
ally. He gives great diligence and pains thereto.
He lives well at his lodging, and gives and spends
liberally, as it beseems his wealth and as his heart

counsels him. The whole Court marvels whence his
store is taken, for he gives to all horses of great price
which he had brought from his land. So much
trouble has Alexander given himself, and so much
has he prevailed by his fair service, that the king
loves and esteems him dearly, and eke the barons
and the queen.

At that point of time King Arthur desired to pass
over into Brittany. He bids all his barons assemble
in order to seek counsel and ask them to whom
till he return he can entrust England, who may
keep and maintain it in peace. By the Council
it was with one consent entrusted, as I think, to
Count Engrés of Windsor, for till then they deemed
no baron more loyal in all the king's land. When
this man had the land in his power, King Arthur
and the queen and her ladies set out on the morrow.
In Brittany folk hear tell that the king and his barons
are coming : the Bretons rejoice greatly thereat.

Into the ship in which the king crossed entered
neither youth nor maiden save Alexander alone, and
the queen of a truth brought thither Soredamors, a
lady who scorned love. Never had she heard tell of
a man whom she could deign to love, however much
beauty, prowess, dominion, or high rank he had.
And yet the damsel was so winsome and fair that she

might well have known love if it had pleased her to
turn her mind to it, but never had she willed to bend
her mind thereto.   Now will Love make her sorrowful,
and Love thinks to avenge himself right well for the
great pride and resistance which she has always
shown to him.   Right well has Love aimed, for he
has stricken her in the heart with his arrow.   Oft
she grows pale, oft the beads of sweat break out,
and in spite of herself she must love.   Scarce can
she refrain from looking towards Alexander, but she
must needs guard herself against my Lord Gawain,
her brother.   Dearly does she buy and pay for her
great pride and her disdain.   Love has heated for her
a bath which mightily inflames and enkindles her.
Now is he kind to her, now cruel;   now she wants
him, and now she rejects him.   She accuses her eyes
of treachery, and says:  "Eyes, you have betrayed
me.   Through you has my heart, which was wont
to be faithful, conceived hatred for me.   Now does
what I see bring grief.   Grief ?   Nay, in truth, but
rather pleasure.   And if I see aught that grieves me,
still have I not my eyes under my own sway ?   My
strength must indeed have failed me, and I must
esteem myself but lightly if I cannot control my eyes
and make them look elsewhere.   By so doing, I shall
be able to guard myself right well from Love, who

wishes to be my master. What the eye sees not the
heart does not lament. If I do not see him, there
will be no pain. He does not entreat or seek me :
if he had loved me, he would have sought me. And
since he neither loves nor esteems me, shall I love him
if he loves me not ? If his beauty draws my eyes,
and my eyes obey the spell, shall I for that say I love
him ? Nay, for that would be a lie. By drawing
my eyes he has done me no wrong of which I can
complain, and I can bring no charge at all against
him. One cannot love with the eyes. And what
wrong, then, have my eyes done to me if they gaze
on what I will to look at ? What fault and wrong
do they commit ? Ought I to blame them ? Nay.
Whom, then? Myself, who have them in my
keeping. My eye looks on nought unless it pleases
and delights my heart. My heart could not wish
for aught that would make me sorrowful. It is
my heart's will that makes me sorrow. Sorrow ?
Faith, then am I mad, since through my heart I desire
that which makes me mad. I ought indeed, if I
can, to rid myself of a will whence grief may come
to me. If I can ? Fool, what have I said ? Then
were I weak indeed if I had no power over myself.
Does Love think to put me in the way which is wont
to mislead other folk ? Thus may he lead others,

but I am not his at all.  Never shall I be so, never
was I so, never shall I desire his further acquaint-
ance."   Thus she disputes with herself, one hour
loves and another hates.  She is in such doubt that
she does not know which side to take.  She thinks
she is defending herself against Love, but she is in
no need of defence.    God!  Why does she not
know that the thoughts of Alexander, on his side, are
directed towards her ?  Love deals out to them
impartially such a portion as is meet for each.  He
gives to them many a reason and ground that the one
should love and desire the other.  This love would
have been loyal and right if the one had known what
was the will of the other ; but he does not know
what she desires, nor she for what he is lamenting.

The queen watches them, and sees the one and the
other often lose colour and grow pale, and sigh and
shudder ; but she knows not why they do it, unless
it be on account of the sea on which they are sailing.
Perhaps, indeed, she would have perceived it if the
sea had not misled her ; but it is the sea which
baffles and deceives her, so that amid the sea-sickness
she sees not the heart-sickness.  For they are at sea,
and heart-sickness is the cause of their plight, and
heart-bitterness is the cause of the malady that grips
them ; but of these three the queen can only blame

the sea; for heart-sickness and heart-bitterness lay the blame on the sea-sickness, and because of the third the two who are guilty get off scot-free. He who is guiltless of fault or wrong often pays dear for the sin of another. Thus the queen violently accuses the sea and blames it; but wrongly is the blame laid on the sea, for the sea has done therein no wrong. Much sorrow has Soredamors borne ere the ship has come to port. The king's coming is noised abroad, for the Bretons had great joy thereof, and served him right willingly as their lawful lord. I seek not to speak more at length of King Arthur at this time: rather shall ye hear me tell how Love torments the two lovers, against whom he has taken the field.

Alexander loves and desires her who is sighing for his love, but he knows not, and will not know aught of this, until he shall have suffered many an ill and many a grief. For love of her he serves the queen and the ladies of her chamber; but he does not dare to speak to or address her who is most in his mind. If she had dared to maintain against him the right which she thinks is hers in the matter, willingly would she have told him of it, but she neither dares nor ought to do so. And the fact that the one sees the other, and that they dare not speak or act, turns to great adversity for them, and love grows thereby and

burns.  But it is the custom of all lovers that they
willingly feed their eyes on looks if they can do no
better, and think that, because the source whence
their love buds and grows delights them, therefore
it must help their case, whereas it injures them :
just as the man who approaches and comes close
to the fire burns himself more than the man who
draws back from it.  Their love grows and increases
continually : but the one feels shame before the
other, and each conceals and hides this love so
that neither flame nor smoke is seen from the gleed
beneath the ashes.  But the heat is none the less for
that, rather the heat lasts longer below the gleed
than above it.  Both the lovers are in very great
anguish ; for in order that their complaint may not
be known or perceived, each must deceive all men
by false pretence ; but in the night great is the
plaint which each makes in solitude.

First will I tell you of Alexander, how he complains
and laments.  Love brings before his mind the lady
for whose sake he feels such sorrow, for she has robbed
him of his heart, and will not let him rest in his bed,
so much it delights him to recall the beauty and the
mien of her as to whom he dare not hope that ever
joy of her may fall to his lot.  " I may hold myself
a fool," quoth he.  " A fool ?  Truly am I a fool,

since I do not dare to say what I think; for quickly would it turn to my bane. I have set my thought on folly. Then is it not better for me to meditate in silence than to get myself dubbed a fool? Never shall my desire be known. And shall I hide the cause of my grief and not dare to seek help or succour for my sorrows? He who is conscious of weakness is a fool if he does not seek that by which he may have health, if he can find it anywhere: but many a one thinks to gain his own advantage and to win what he desires who pursues that whereof he sorrows later. And why should he go to seek advice when he does not expect to find health? That were a vain toil! I feel my own ill so heavy a burden that never shall I find healing for it by medicine, or by potion, or by herb, or by root. There is not a remedy for every ill: mine is so rooted that it cannot be cured. Cannot? Methinks I have lied. As soon as I first felt this evil, if I had dared to reveal and to tell it, I could have spoken to a leech, who could have helped me in the whole matter; but it is very grievous for me to speak out. Perhaps they would not deign to listen, and would refuse to accept a fee. No wonder is it then if I am dismayed; for I have a great ill, and yet I do not know what ill it is which sways me, nor do I know whence comes this pain. I do not know?

Yes, indeed, I think I know; Love makes me feel
this evil. How? Does Love, then, know how to
do evil? Is he not kind and debonair? I thought
that there would have been nought in love which was
not good; but I have found him very malicious.
He who has not put him to the test knows not with
what games Love meddles. He is a fool who goes
to meet him, for always he wishes to burden his
subjects. Faith! his game is not at all a good one.
It is ill playing with him, for his sport will cause
me sorrow. What shall I do, then? Shall I draw
back? I think that this would be the act of a wise
man; but I cannot tell how to set about it. If
Love chastises and threatens in order to teach me his
lesson, ought I to disdain my master? He who
despises his master is a fool. Needs must I store up
in my mind Love's lesson, for soon can great good
come of it. But he buffets me greatly: that sets me
in alarm! True, neither blow nor wound is visible,
and yet dost thou complain? Then art thou not
wrong? Nay, indeed; for he has wounded me so
sore that he has winged his arrow even to my heart,
and not yet has he drawn it out again. How then
has he struck his dart into thy body, when no wound
appears without? This shalt thou tell me; I would
fain know it. In what member has he struck thee?

Through the eye.  Through the eye?  And yet he has not put out thine eye?  He has done me no hurt in the eye, but he wounds me sorely at the heart. Now speak reason to me:  how has the dart passed through thine eye in such wise that the eye is not wounded or bruised by it?  If the dart enter through the midst of the eye, why does my heart suffer pain in my body?  Why does not my eye also feel the pain, since it receives the first blow?  That can I well explain.  The eye has no care to understand aught, nor can it do anything in the matter in any way; but the eye is the mirror to the heart, and through this mirror passes the fire by which the heart is kindled, yet so that it neither wounds nor bruises it.  Then is not the heart placed in the body like the lighted candle which is put inside the lantern?  If you take the candle out, never will any light issue thence; but as long as the candle lasts the lantern is not dark, and the flame which shines through neither harms nor injures it. Likewise is it with regard to a window:  never will it be so strong and so whole but that the ray of the sun may pass through it without hurting it in any way; and the glass will never be so clear that one will see any better for its brightness, if another brightness does not strike upon it.  Know that it is the same with the eyes as with the glass and the lantern; for the light penetrates into the eyes, the heart's mirror, and the heart sees the object outside, whatever it be, and sees many various objects, some green, others dark of hue, one crimson, the other blue, and it blames the one and praises the other, holds the one cheap and the other precious; but many an object shows him a fair face in the mirror when he looks at it, which will betray him if he be not on his guard. My mirror has much deceived me, for in it my heart has seen a ray by which I am struck, which has taken shelter in me; and because of this my heart has failed me. I am ill-treated by my friend, who deserts me for my enemy. Well can I accuse my mirror of treachery, for it has sinned exceedingly against me. I thought I had three friends, my heart and my two eyes together; but methinks they hate me. Where shall I find any more a friend, since these three are enemies, who belong to me yet kill me? My servants presume overmuch, who do all their own will and have no care of mine. Now know I well, of a truth, from the action of those who have injured me, that a good master's love decays through keeping bad servants. He who associates with a bad servant cannot fail to lament it sooner or later, whatever come of it.

"Now will I speak to you again of the arrow

which is given in trust to me, and tell you how it is
made and cut; but I fear much that I may fail in
the matter, for the carved work of it is so magnificent
that 'twill be no marvel if I fail.   And yet I will apply
all my diligence to say what I think of it.   The notch
and the feathers together are so close, if a man looks
well at them, that there is but one dividing line like
a narrow parting in the hair; but this line is so polished
and straight, that without question there is nought in
the notch which can be improved.   The feathers are of
such a hue as if they were gold or gilded, but gilding can
add nothing ; for the feathers, this know I well, were
brighter still than gold.   The feathers are the blonde
tresses that I saw the other day at sea.   This is the
arrow that makes me love.   God !   What a price-
less boon !   If a man could have such a treasure,
why should he desire any other wealth all his life ?
For my part, I could swear that I should desire
nothing more ; for merely the feathers and the notch
would I not give away in exchange for Antioch.   And
since I prize these two things so much, who could
duly appraise the value of the rest, which is so fair
and lovable, and so dear and so precious, that I am
desirous and eager to behold myself mirrored again
in the brow that God has made so bright that nor
mirror nor emerald nor topaz would make any show

beside it. But of all this he who gazes at the bright-
ness of the eyes has not a word to say, for to all those
who behold them they seem two glowing candles.
And who has so glib a tongue that he could describe
the fashion of the well-shaped nose and of the bright
countenance, where the rose overlays the lily so
that it eclipses something of the lily in order the better
to illuminate the face; and of the smiling little
mouth, which God made such on purpose that no
one should see it and not think that it is laughing?
And what of the teeth in her mouth? One is so
close to the other that it seems that they all touch;
and so that they might the better achieve this, Nature
bestowed special pains, so that whoever should see
them when the mouth opens would never dream
that they were not of ivory or silver. So much there
is to say and to recount in the describing of each
thing—both of the chin and of the ears—that it would
be no great marvel if I were to leave out something.
Of the throat, I tell you that in comparison with it
crystal is but dim. And the neck beneath her tresses
is four times whiter than ivory. As much as is dis-
closed from the hem of the vest behind to the clasp
of the opening in front saw I of the bare bosom un-
covered, whiter than is the new-fallen snow. My
pain would indeed have been alleviated if I could

have seen the whole of the arrow. Right willingly, if I had known, would I have said what the tip of the arrow is like : I did not see it, and it is not my own fault if I cannot tell the fashion of a thing that I have not seen. Love showed me then nought of it except the notch and the feathers ; for the arrow was put in the quiver : the quiver is the tunic and the vest wherewith the maid was clad. Faith ! this is the wound that kills me, this is the dart, this is the ray with which I am so cruelly inflamed. It is ignoble of me to be angry ; never for provocation or for war shall any pledge that I must seek of love be broken. Now let Love dispose of me, as he ought to do with what is his ; for I wish it, and this is my pleasure. Never do I seek that this malady should leave me : rather do I wish it to hold me thus for ever, and that from none may health come to me if health come not from that source whence the disease has come."

Great is the plaint of Alexander, but that which the damsel utters is not a whit less. All night she is in so great pain that she neither sleeps nor rests. Love has set in array within her a battle that rages and mightily agitates her heart, and which causes such anguish and torture that she weeps all night, and complains and tosses and starts up, so that her heart all but stops beating. And when she has so grieved, and sobbed, and moaned, and started, and sighed, then she has looked in her heart to see who and of what worth was he for whose sake Love was torturing her.  And when she has recalled each wandering thought, then she stretches herself and turns over;  and turning, she turns to folly all the thinking she has done.   Then she starts on another argument, and says : " Fool!  what does it matter to me if this youth is debonair, and wise, and courteous, and valiant ?   All this is honour and advantage to him.   And what care I for his beauty ?   Let his beauty depart with him,—and so it will, for all I can do ;  never would I wish to take away aught of it.  Take away ?   Nay truly, that do I not assuredly.   If he had the wisdom of Solomon, and if Nature had put so much beauty in him that she could not have put more in a human body, and if God had put in my hand the power to destroy all, I would not seek to anger him, but willingly, if I could, would I make him more wise and more beautiful.   Faith ! then I do not hate him at all.   And am I then on that account his lady ?   No, indeed ;  no more than I am another's.   And wherefore do I think more of him if he does not please me more than another ? I know not : I am all bewildered ; for never did I think so much about any man living in the world.

And if I had my wish I should see him always; never
would I seek to take my eyes off him, so much
the sight of him delights me. Is this love? Me-
thinks it is. Never should I have called on him so
often if I had not loved him more than another.
Yes, I love him: let that be granted. And shall I
not have my desire? Yes, provided that I find
favour in his eyes. This desire is wrong; but Love
has taken such hold of me that I am foolish and dazed,
and to defend myself avails me nought herein; thus
I must suffer Love's attack. I have indeed guarded
myself thus wisely and for long against Love, never
once before did I wish to do aught for him; but
now I am too gracious to him. And what thanks
does he owe me, since he cannot have service or kind-
ness of me by fair means? It is by force that Love
has tamed my pride, and I must needs be subject to
his will. Now I wish to love, now I am under his
tuition, now will Love teach me. And what? How
I ought to serve him. Of that am I right well ap-
prised. I am full wise in his service, for no one could
find fault with me in this matter. No need is there
henceforth for me to learn more. Love would have
me, and I would fain be, wise, without pride, gracious
and courteous towards all, but the true love of one
only. Shall I love them all for the sake of one? A

fair mien should I show to each, but Love does
not bid me to be a true love to every man.  Love
teaches nought but good.  It is not for nothing that
I have this name, and that I am called Soredamors.
I ought to love and I ought to be loved, and I wish
to prove it by my name, if I can find fitting argu-
ments.  It is not without meaning that the first part
of my name is the colour of gold; for the most
beautiful are the blondest.  Therefore I hold my name
the fairer, because it begins with the colour with
which accords the finest gold.  And the end recalls
Love, for he who calls me by my right name ever calls
love to my mind.  And the one half gilds the other
with bright and yellow gilding; for Soredamors
means the same thing as 'gilded with love.'  Much,
then, has Love honoured me, since he has gilded me
with himself.  Gilding of gold is not so fine as that
which illumines me.  And I shall set my care on this,
that I may be of his gilding; nevermore will I complain
of him.  Now I love, and shall always love.  Whom ?
Truly, a fine question !  Him whom Love bids me
love, for no other shall ever have my love.  What does
it matter, as he will never know it, unless I tell him
myself ?  What shall I do if I do not pray him for
his love ?  For he who desires a thing ought indeed
to request and pray for it.  How ?   Shall I then

pray him ? Nay, indeed. Why not ? It never
happened that a woman did aught so witless as to
beg a man for love, unless she were more than common
mad. I should be convicted of folly if I said with
my mouth aught that might turn to my reproach. If
he should know it from my mouth, I deem that he
would hold me the cheaper for it, and would often
reproach me with having been the first to pray for
love. Never be love so abased that I should go and
entreat this man, since he would be bound to hold
me the cheaper for it. Ah God ! how will he ever
know it, since I shall not tell him ? As yet I have
scarce suffered aught for which I need so distress my-
self. I shall wait till he perceives, if he is ever destined
to perceive it. He will know it well, of a truth, I
think, if ever he had aught to do with love or heard
tell of it by word of mouth. Heard tell ? Now
have I said foolish words. Love's lore is not so easy
that a man becomes wise by speaking of it, unless
good experience be there too. Of myself I know this
well ; for never could I learn aught of it by fair
speaking or by word of mouth, and yet I have been
much at Love's school and have often been flattered ;
but always have I kept aloof from him, and now he
makes me pay dear for it ; for now I know more of
it than an ox does of ploughing. But of this I despair

—that he never loved perhaps; and if he does not love and has not loved, then have I been sowing in the sea, where no seed can take root; and there is nothing for it but to wait for him, and to suffer till I see whether I can bring him into the right way by hints and covert words. I will so act that he will be certain of having my love if he dares to seek it. Thus the end of the whole matter is that I love him and am his. If he does not love me, I shall love him all the same."

Thus both he and she complain, and the one hides the case from the other; they have sorrow in the night, and worse by day. In such pain they have, it seems to me, been a long while in Brittany, until it came to the end of summer. Right at the beginning of October came messengers from the parts about Dover, from London and from Canterbury, to bring the king tidings that have troubled his heart. The messengers have told him this—that he may well tarry too long in Brittany; for he to whom he had entrusted his land and had consigned so great a host of his subjects and of his friends will now set himself in battle array against the king, and he has marched into London in order to hold the city against the hour that Arthur should have returned.

When the king heard the news, he calls all his barons;

for he was indignant and full of displeasure. That
he may the better stir them up to confound the
traitor, he says that all the blame for his toil and
for his war is theirs ; for through their persuasion
he gave his land and put it into the hand of the
traitor, who is worse than Ganelon. There is not
one who does not quite allow that the king has right
and reason ; for they all counselled him to do so ;
but the traitor will be ruined for it. And let him
know well, of a truth, that in no castle or city will
he be able so to protect his body that they do not
drag him out of it by force. Thus they all assure
the king, and solemnly affirm and swear that they
will give up the traitor or no longer hold their lands.
And the king has it proclaimed through all Brittany
that none who can bear arms in the host remain in
the country without coming after him quickly.

All Brittany is moved : never was such a host seen
as King Arthur assembled. When the ships moved
out, it seemed that everybody in the world was on
the sea ; for not even the waves were seen, so covered
were they with ships. This fact is certain, that it
seems from the stir that all Brittany is taking ship.
Now have the ships made the passage, and the folk who
have thronged together go into quarters along the
shore. It came into Alexander's heart to go and beg

the king to make him a knight, for if ever he is to
win renown he will win it in this war. He takes his
comrades with him, as his will urges him on to do
what he has purposed. They have gone to the
king's tent: the king was sitting before his tent.
When he sees the Greeks coming, he has called them
before him. "Sirs," quoth he, "hide not from
me what need brought you here." Alexander spake
for all, and has told him his desire: "I am come,"
quoth he, "to pray you, as I am bound to pray my
lord, for my companions and for myself that you make
us knights." The king replies: "Right gladly, and
not a moment's delay shall there be, since you have
made me this request." Then the king bids there
be borne harness for twelve knights: done is what
the king commands. Each asks for his own harness,
and each has his own in his possession, fair arms and
a good steed: each one has taken his harness. All
the twelve were of like value, arms and apparel and
horse; but the harness for Alexander's body was
worth as much—if any one had cared to value or to
sell it—as the arms of all the other twelve together.
Straightway by the sea they disrobed and washed and
bathed; for they neither wished nor deigned that
any other bath should be heated for them. They
made the sea their bath and tub.

The queen, who does not hate Alexander—rather does she love and praise and prize him much—hears of the matter. She wills to do him a great service; it is far greater than she thinks. She searches and empties all her chests till she has drawn forth a shirt of white silk, very well wrought, very delicate, and very fine. There was no thread in the seams that was not of gold or at the least of silver. Soredamors from time to time had set her hands to the sewing, and had in places sewn in, beside the gold, a hair from her head both on the two sleeves and on the collar, to see and to put to the test whether she could ever find a man who could distinguish the one from the other, however carefully he looked at it; for the hair was as shining and as golden as the gold, or even more so. The queen takes the shirt, and has given it to Alexander. Ah God! how great joy would Alexander have had if he had known what the queen is sending him. Very great joy would she too have had who had sewn her hair there, if she had known that her love was to have and wear it. Much comfort would she have had thereof; for she would not have loved all the rest of her hair so much as that which Alexander had. But neither he nor she knew it: great pity is it that they do not know. To the harbour, where the youths are washing, came the

messenger of the queen ; he finds the youths on the
beach, and has given the shirt to him who is much
delighted with it, and who held it all the dearer for
that it came from the queen.  But if he had known
the whole case, he would have loved it still more ; for
he would not have taken all the world in exchange,
but rather he would have treated it as a relic, as I
think, and would have worshipped it day and night.

Alexander delays no longer to apparel himself
straightway.  When he was clad and equipped, he
has returned to the tent of the king, and all his
comrades together with him.  The queen, as I think,
had come to sit in the tent, because she wished to
see the new knights arrive.  Well might one esteem
them fair ; but fairest of all was Alexander with the
agile body.  They are now knights ; for the present
I say no more about them.  Henceforth shall I speak
of the king and of the host which came to London.
The greater part of the folk held to his side, but
there is a great multitude of them against him.
Count Engrés musters his troops, all that he can
win over to him by promise or by gift.  When
he had got his men together, he has secretly fled by
night, for he was hated by several and feared to be
betrayed ; but before he fled he took from London as
much as he could of victuals, of gold, and of silver,
and distributed it all to his folk.  The tidings is told

to the king—that the traitor is fled and all his army
with him, and that he had taken so much of victuals
and goods from the city that the burgesses are im-
poverished and destitute and at a loss.  And the king
has replied just this: that never will he take ransom of
the traitor, but will hang him if he can find or take
him.  Now all the host bestirs itself so much that they
reached Windsor.  At that day, however it be now, if
any one wished to defend the castle, it would not have
been easy to take ; for the traitor enclosed it, as soon
as he planned the treason, with treble walls and moats,
and had strengthened the walls behind with sharpened
stakes so that they should not be thrown down by any
siege-engine.  He had spent great sums in strengthen-
ing it all June and July and August, in making walls,
and abattis, and moats, and drawbridges, trenches,
and breastworks, and barriers, and many a portcullis
of iron, and a great tower of stones hewn foursquare.
Never had he shut the gate there for fear of attack.
The castle stands on a high hill, and below it runs
Thames. ˙ The host is encamped on the river-bank ;
on that day they had time for nought save encamping
and pitching their tents.

The host has encamped on Thames: all the
meadow is covered with tents, green and vermilion.
The sun strikes on the colours, and the river reflects

their sheen for more than a full league. The defenders
of the castle had come to take their pleasure along
the strand, with their lances only in their hands, their
shields locked close in front of them ; for they bore
no arms but these. To their foes without they
made it appear that they feared them not at all,
inasmuch as they had come unarmed. Alexander, on
the other side, perceived the knights who go before
them, playing a knightly game on horseback. Hot
is his desire to meet with them, and he calls
his comrades one after the other by their names.
First Cornix, whom he greatly loved, then the stout
Licorides, then Nabunal of Mycenæ, and Acoriondes
of Athens, and Ferolin of Salonica, and Calcedor from
towards Africa, Parmenides and Francagel, Torin the
Strong, and Pinabel, Nerius, and Neriolis. "Lords,"
quoth he, "a longing has seized me to go and make
with lance and with shield acquaintance with those
who come to tourney before us. I see full well that
they take us for laggards and esteem us lightly—so
it seems to me—since they have come here all un-
armed to tourney before our faces. We have been
newly dubbed knights ; we have not yet shown our
mettle to knights or at quintain. Too long have
we kept our new lances virgin. Why were our shields
made ? Not yet have they been pierced or broken

Such a gift avails us nought save for stour or for assault.
Let us pass the ford, and let us attack them." All
say : " We will not fail you." Each one says : " So
may God save me, as I am not the man to fail you
here." Now they gird on their swords, saddle and
girth their steeds, mount and take their shields.
When they had hung the shields from their necks
and taken the lances blazoned in quarterings, they
all at once rush on to the ford, and the enemy lower
their lances and ride quickly to strike them. But
Alexander and his comrades knew well how to pay
them back, and they neither spare them nor shirk
nor yield a foot before them ; rather each strikes his
own foe so doughtily that there is no knight so good
but he must void his saddle-bow. The Greeks did
not take them for boys, for cowards, or for men
bewildered. They have not wasted their first blows,
for they have unhorsed thirteen. The noise of their
blows and strokes has reached as far as to the army.
In a short time the mellay would have been desperate,
if the enemy had dared to stand before them. The
king's men run through the host to take their weapons,
and dash into the water noisily : and the enemy
turn to flight, for they see that it is not good to stay
there. And the Greeks follow them, striking with
lances and swords. Many heads there were cut

open; but of the Greeks there was not a single one
wounded.  They have proved themselves well that day.
But Alexander won the greatest distinction, for he
leads away four knights bound to his person and taken
prisoners.  And the dead lie on the strand, for many
there lay headless, and many wounded and maimed.

Alexander from courtesy gives and presents the
firstfruits of his knighthood to the queen.  He does
not wish that the king should have possession of the
captives, for he would have had them all hanged.
Then queen has had them taken, and has had them
guarded in prison as accused of treason.  Men speak
of the Greeks throughout the army; all say that
Alexander is right courteous and debonair as regards
the knights whom he had taken, inasmuch as he had
not given them up to the king, who would have had
them burned or hanged.  But the king is in earnest
in the matter.  Forthwith he bids the queen that
she come and speak to him and keep not her traitors,
for it will behove her to give them up, or he will
take them against her will.  Then queen has come to
the king, they have had converse together about the
traitors as it behoved them, and all the Greeks had
been left in the queen's tent with the ladies.  Much
do the twelve say to them; but Alexander does
not say a word.  Soredamors observed it; she had

sat down near him. He has rested his cheek on his hand, and it seems that he is deep in thought. Thus have they sat full long, till Soredamors saw on his arm and at his neck the hair with which she had made the seam. She has drawn a little nearer him, for now she has opportunity of speaking with him; but she considers beforehand how she can be the one to speak, and what the first word shall be, whether she will call him by his name; and she takes counsel of it with herself. "What shall I say first?" thinks she. "Shall I address him by his name, or as 'friend'? Friend? Not I. How then? Call him by his name? God! the word friend is so fair and so sweet to say. What if I dared to call him friend? Dared? What forbids it me? The fact that I think I should be telling a lie. A lie? I know not what it will be; but if I lie, it will be a weight on my mind. For that reason it must be allowed that I should not desire to lie in the matter. God! he would not lie now a whit if he called me his sweet friend. And should I lie in so calling him? Both of us ought indeed to speak truth; but if I lie, the wrong will be his. And why is his name so hard to me that I wish to add a name of courtesy? It seems to me there are too many letters in it, and I should become tongue-tied in the middle. But if I called him friend

I should very quickly say this name.   But just because I fear to stumble in the other name, I would have given of my heart's-blood if only his name might have been ' my sweet friend.' "

She delays so long in thus thinking that the queen returns from the king, who had sent for her.   Alexander sees her coming, and goes to meet her, and asks her what the king commands to be done with his prisoners, and what will be their fate.   " Friend," says she, " he requires me to yield them up to his discretion, and to let him do his justice on them.   He is very wroth that I have not yet given them up to him ; and I must send them, for I see no other way out."   Thus they have passed this day, and on the morrow the good and loyal knights have assembled together before the royal tent to pronounce justice and judgment, as to with what penalty and with what torture the four traitors should die.   Some doom that they be flayed, others that they be hanged or burnt ; and the king himself deems that traitors should be drawn.   Then he bids them be brought : they are brought ; he has them bound, and tells them that they shall not be quartered till they are in view of the castle, so that those within shall see them.

When the parley is done, the king addresses Alexander, and calls him his dear friend.   " Friend,"

quoth he, " I saw you yesterday make a fair attack
and a fair defence. I will give you the due guerdon :
I increase your following by 500 Welsh knights and
by 1000 footmen of this land. When I shall have
finished my war, in addition to what I have given
you I will have you crowned king of the best realm
in Wales. Market-towns and strong castles, cities
and halls will I give you meanwhile, till the land
shall be given to you which your father holds, and
of which you must become emperor." Alexander
heartily thanks the king for this grant, and his
comrades thank him likewise. All the barons of the
Court say that the honour which the king designs for
him is well vested in Alexander.

When Alexander sees his men, his comrades and
his footmen, such as the king willed to give him, then
they begin to sound horns and trumpets throughout
the host. Good and bad all, I would have you
know, without exception, take their arms, those of
Wales and of Brittany, of Scotland and of Cornwall ;
for from all sides without fail strong reinforcements
had come in for the host. Thames had shrunk ; for
there had been no rain all the summer, rather there
had been such a drought that the fish in it were
dead and the ships leaky in the harbour, and one
could pass by ford there where the water was widest.

The host has crossed Thames; some beset the
valley, and others mount the height. The defenders
of the castle perceive it, and see coming the
wondrous host which is preparing outside to over-
throw and take the castle, and they prepare to defend
it. But before any attack is made, the king has the
traitors dragged by four horses round the castle,
through the valleys and over mounds and hillocks.
Count Engrés is sore grieved when he sees those
whom he held dear dragged round his castle, and the
others were much dismayed; but for all the dismay
that they feel thereat, they have no desire to surrender.
Needs must they defend themselves; for the king
displays openly to all his displeasure and his wrath,
and full well they see that if he held them he would
make them die shamefully.

When the four had been drawn and their limbs
lay o'er the field, then the attack begins; but all
their toil is vain, for howsoever they may hurl
and throw their missiles they can avail nought. And
yet they try hard; they throw and hurl a thick
cloud of bolts and javelins and darts. The catapults
and slings make a great din on all sides; arrows and
round stone fly likewise in confusion as thick as rain
mingled with hail. Thus they toil all day: these
defend and those attack, until night separates them.

And the king, on his part, has it cried through the host and made known what gift that man will have of him by whom the castle shall have been taken: a goblet of very great price, worth fifteen golden marks, the richest in his treasure, will he give him. The goblet will be very fair and rich, and he whose judgment goes not astray ought to hold it dearer for the workmanship than for the material. The goblet is very precious in workmanship, and, if I were to disclose the whole truth, the jewels on the outside were worth more than the workmanship or the gold. If he by whom the castle will be taken is but a foot-soldier, he shall have the cup. And if it is taken by a knight, never shall he seek any reward besides the cup, but he will have it, if it can be found in the world.

When this matter was proclaimed, Alexander, who went each evening to see the queen, had not forgotten his custom. On this evening he had again gone thither; they were seated side by side, both Alexander and the queen. Before them Soredamors was sitting alone nearest to them, and she looked at him as gladly as though she would not have preferred to be in Paradise. The queen held Alexander by his right hand, and looked at the golden thread, which had become greatly tarnished, and the hair was becoming

yet fairer whereas the gold thread was growing pale ;
and she remembered by chance that Soredamors had
done the stitching, and she laughed thereat. Alexander
observed it, and asks her, if it may be told, to tell
him what makes her laugh. The queen delays to
tell him, and looks towards Soredamors, and has
called her before her. She has come very gladly, and
kneels before her. Alexander was much joyed when
he saw her approach so near that he could have touched
her, but he has not so much courage as to dare even to
look at her, but all his senses have so left him that he
has almost become dumb. And she, on the other hand,
is so bewildered that she has no use of her eyes, but
fixes her gaze on the ground, and dares not direct it
elsewhere. The queen greatly marvels ; she sees
her now pale now flushed, and notes well in her
heart the bearing and appearance of each and of the
two together. She sees clearly and truly, it seems
to her, judging by the changes of colour, that these
are signs of love ; but she does not wish to cause
them anguish : she feigns to know nothing of what
she sees. She did just what it behoved her to do, for
she gave no look or hint, save that she said to the
maiden : "Damsel, look yonder and tell—hide it
not from us—where the shirt that this knight has
donned was sewn, and whether you had a hand in

it and put in it somewhat of yours ? " The maiden
is ashamed to say it, nevertheless she tells it to him
gladly; for she wishes that he should hear the truth;
and he has such joy of hearing it, when she tells and
describes to him the making of the shirt, that with
great difficulty he restrains himself, when he sees the
hair, from worshipping and doing reverence to it.
His comrades and the queen, who were there with
him, cause him great distress and annoyance, for on
account of them he refrains from raising it to his
eyes and to his lips, where he would fain have pressed
it, if he had not thought that they would see him.
He is blithe that he has so much of his lady-love;
but he does not think or expect to have ever any other
boon of her. His desire makes him fear; neverthe-
less, when he is alone he kisses it more than a hundred
thousand times, when he has left the queen.
Now it seems to him that he was born in a lucky
hour. Very great joy does he have of it all night,
but he takes good care that no one sees him. When
he has lain down in his bed, he delights and consoles
him fruitlessly with that in which there is no delight;
all night he embraces the shirt, and when he beholds
the hair, he thinks he is lord of all the world. Truly
love makes a wise man a fool, since he has joy
of a hair and has delight and joyaunce thereof; but

he will change his pastime before the bright dawn
and the sunlight. The traitors are holding counsel
as to what they will be able to do and what will
become of them. Long time they will be able to
defend the castle, that is a certainty, if they apply
themselves to the defence; but they know that the
king is of so fierce a courage that in all his life he
will never turn away until he has taken it;
then they must needs die. And if they surrender
the castle, they expect no grace for that. Thus
the one lot or the other, it has fallen out ill for them,
for they have no reinforcement, and they see death
on all sides. But the end of their deliberation is
that to-morrow, before day appears, they resolve to
issue forth secretly from the castle, and to fall on
the host unarmed and the knights asleep, since they
will still be lying in their beds. Before these have
awakened, apparelled and equipped themselves, they
will have made such slaughter that ever hereafter
shall be related the battle of that night. To this
plan all the traitors cling from desperation, for they
have no confidence as to their lives. Lack of hope
as to the outcome emboldens them to the battle;
for they see no issue for themselves except through
death or prison. Such an issue is no wholesome
one, nor need they trouble to flee, nor do they see

where they could find refuge if they should have
fled; for the sea and their enemies are around
them, and they in the midst. No longer do they
tarry at their council: now they apparel and arm
themselves, and issue forth towards the north-west
by an ancient postern towards that side whence
they thought that those of the host would least expect
to see them come. In serried ranks they sallied forth :
of their men they made five battalions, and there
were no less than two thousand foot-soldiers well
equipped for battle, and a thousand knights in each.
This night neither star nor moon had shown its
rays in the sky; but before they had reached the
tents, the moon began to rise, and I believe that
just to vex them it rose earlier than it was wont,
and God, who wished to injure them, lit up the dark
night; for He had no care of their army, rather He
hated them for their sin with which they were tainted ;
for traitors and treason God hates more than any
other crime; so the moon began to shine, because
it was doomed to injure them.

The moon was veritably hostile to them, for it
shone on their glittering shields, and the helmets
likewise greatly embarrass them, for they reflect the
light of the moon; for the sentries who were set
to guard the host see them, and they cry throughout

all the host : " Up, knights ! Up, rise quickly ! Take
your arms, arm yourselves ! Behold the traitors
upon us ! " Through all the host they spring to
arms ; they rouse themselves and don with haste
their harness, as men must do in case of stress. Never
did a single one of them stir forth till they were fully
equipped and all mounted on their steeds. While
they are arming, the enemy, on the other hand, who
greatly desire the battle, are bestirring themselves,
so that they may take them unawares and likewise find
them unarmed ; and they send forth their men, whom
they had divided into five bands. Some kept beside
the wood, others came along the river, the third placed
themselves in the plain, and the fourth were in a valley,
and the fifth battalion spurs along the moat that sur-
rounded a rock ; for they thought to swoop down im-
petuously among the tents. But they have not found
a road that they could follow or a way that was not
barred ; for the king's men block their way, as they very
proudly defy them and reproach them with treason.
They engage with the iron heads of their lances, so
that they splinter and break them ; they come to
close quarters with swords, and champion strikes
champion to the ground and makes him bite the
dust ; each side strikes down its foes ; and, as
fiercely as lions, devouring whatsoever they can

seize, rush on their prey, so fiercely do they rush on
their foe—aye, and more fiercely. On both sides, of
a truth, there was very great loss of life at that first
attack; but reinforcements come for the traitors,
who defend themselves very fiercely and sell their
lives dear when they can keep them no longer. On
four sides they see their battalions coming to succour
them; and the king's men gallop upon them as fast
as they can spur. They rush to deal them such blows
on the shields that, together with the wounded, they
have overthrown more than five hundred of them.
The Greeks spare them not at all. Alexander is not
idle; for he exerts himself to act bravely. In the
thickest of the fray he rushes so impetuously to smite
a traitor, that neither shield nor hauberk availed one
whit to save that traitor from being thrown to the
ground. When Alexander has made a truce with
him forsooth, he pays his attentions to another—
attentions in which he does not waste or lose his
pains. He serves him in such valiant sort that he
rends his soul from his body, and the house remains
without a tenant. After these two, Alexander picks
a quarrel with a third: he strikes a right noble courtly
knight through both flanks in such wise that the blood
gushes out of the wound on the opposite side, and
the soul takes leave of the body, for the foeman has

breathed it forth. Many a one he kills, many a one he maims; for like the forked lightning he attacks all those that he seeks out. Him whom he strikes with lance or sword neither corselet nor shield protects. His comrades also are very lavish in spilling blood and brains; well do they know how to deal their blows. And the king's men cut down so many that they break and scatter them like common folk distraught. So many dead lie o'er the fields, and so long has the stour lasted, that the battle-array was broken up a long while before it was day, and the line of dead down along the river extended five leagues.

Count Engrés leaves his standard in the battle and steals away, and he has taken seven of his companions together with him. He has returned towards his castle by so hidden a way that he thinks that no one sees; but Alexander marks him, for he sees them flee from the host, and thinks to steal away and meet them, so that no one will know where he has gone. But before he was in the valley, he saw as many as thirty knights coming after him along a path, six of whom were Greeks and the other four-and-twenty Welsh; for they thought that they would follow him at a distance, until it should come to the pinch. When Alexander perceived them, he stopped to wait, and marks which way those who are returning to the castle take, until he sees them enter. Then he begins to meditate on a very hazardous venture and on a very wondrous stratagem. And when he had finished all his thinking, he turns towards his comrades, and thus has related and said to them: "Lords," quoth he, "without gainsaying me, if ye wish to have my love, whether it be prompted by folly or wisdom, grant me my wish." And they have granted it, for never will they refuse him anything that he may choose to do. "Let us change our insignia," quoth he; "let us take shields and lances from the traitors that we have slain. Thus we shall go towards the castle, and the traitors within will think that we are of their party and, whatever the requital may be, the doors will be opened to us. Know ye in what wise we shall requite them? We shall take them all or dead or living, if God grant it us; and if any of you repent you, know that as long as I live I shall never love him with a good heart."

All grant him his will: they go and seize the shields from the dead, and they arrive with this equipment. And the folk of the castle had mounted to the battlements of the tower, for they recognised the shields full well, and think that they belong to their own men; for they were unsuspicious of the ambush which lurks beneath the shields. The porter

opens the door to them, and has received them within.
He is so beguiled and deceived that he does not address
them at all; and not one of them breathes a word,
but they pass on mute and silent, feigning such grief
that they drag their lances behind them and bend
beneath their shields, so that it seems that they are
sorrowing greatly; and they go in whatever direction
they wish, until they have passed the three walls.
Up yonder they find many foot-soldiers and knights
with the count, I cannot tell you the number of
them; but they were all unarmed, except the eight
alone who had returned from the army, and these
even were preparing to take off their armour. But
they might well prove over-hasty, for those who
have come upon them up yonder no longer hid
themselves, but put their steeds to the gallop. All
press on their stirrups, and fall upon them and attack
them, so that they strike dead thirty-and-one before
they have given the challenge. The traitors are much
dismayed thereat, and cry, " Betrayed! betrayed! "
But Alexander and his friends are not confused, for,
as soon as they find them all unarmed, they test
their swords well there. Even three of those
whom they found armed have they so served that
they have only left five. Count Engrés has rushed
forward, and before the eyes of all goes to strike

Calcedor on his golden shield, so that he throws him
to the ground dead. Alexander is much grieved
when he sees his comrade slain; he well-nigh goes
mad with the fury that comes upon him. His reason
is dimmed with anger, but his strength and courage
are doubled, and he goes to strike the count with
such a mighty force that his lance breaks, for willingly,
if he could, would he avenge the death of his friend.
But the count was of great strength, a good and bold
knight to boot, such that there would not have been
a better in the world if he had not been disloyal and
a traitor. The count, on his side, prepares to give
him such a blow that he bends his lance, so that it
altogether splinters and breaks; but the shield does
not break, and the one knight does not shake the other
from his seat any more than he would have shaken
a rock, for both were very strong. But the fact that
the count was in the wrong mightily vexes and
weakens him. The one grows furious against the
other, and both have drawn their swords since they
had broken their lances. And there would have
been no escape, if these two champions had wished
further to prolong the fight; one or the other
would have had to die forthwith at the end.
But the count does not dare to stand his ground,
for he sees his men slain around him, who, being

unarmed, were taken unawares. And the king's men
pursue them fiercely, and hack and hew, and cleave,
and brain them, and call the count a traitor. When
he hears himself accused of treason, he flies for refuge
towards his keep, and his men flee with him. And
their enemies, who fiercely rush after, take them cap-
tive; they let not a single one escape of all those that
they catch. They kill and slay so many, that I do not
think that more than seven reached a place of safety.

When the traitors entered the keep, they are
stayed at the entrance; for their pursuers had
followed them so close that their men would have got
in if the entrance had been open. The traitors defend
themselves well, for they expect succour from their
men, who were arming in the town below. But by
the advice of Nabunal, a Greek who was very wise, the
way was held against the reinforcements, so that
they could not come in time, for they had tarried
over-long from lukewarmness and indolence. Up
there into that fortress there was only one single
entry; if the Greeks stop up that entrance, they
will have no need to fear the coming of any force
from which ill may befall them. Nabunal bids and
exhorts that twenty of them go to defend the outer
gateway, for easily there might press in that way,
to attack and overwhelm them, foemen who would do

them harm, if they had strength and power to do so. Let a score of men go to defend the gateway, and let the other ten assail the keep from without, so that the count may not shut himself up inside. Done is what Nabunal advises : the ten remain in the mellay before the entrance of the keep, the score go to the gate. They have delayed almost too long, for they see coming a company flushed and heated with desire of fighting, in which there were many crossbowmen and foot-soldiers of divers equipments, bearing divers arms. Some carried light missiles, and others Danish axes, Turkish lances and swords, arrows, and darts, and javelins. Very heavy would have been the reckoning that the Greeks would have had to pay, peradventure, if this company had come upon them ; but they did not come in time. By the wisdom and by the prudence of Nabunal, they forestalled them and kept them without. When the reinforcements see that they are shut out, then they remain idle, for they see well that by attacking they will be able to accomplish nought in the matter. Then there rises a mourning and a cry of women and of little children, of old men and of youths, so great that if it had thundered from the sky those within the castle would not have heard aught of it. The Greeks greatly rejoice thereat, for now they all know of a surety that never by any chance

will the count escape being taken. They bid four
of them mount in haste to the battlements of the
wall to see that those without do not from any quarter,
by any stratagem or trick, press into the castle to attack
them. The sixteen have returned to the ten who
are fighting. Now was it bright daylight, and now
the ten had forced their way into the keep; and the
count, armed with an axe, had taken his stand beside
a pillar, where he defends himself right fiercely. He
cleaves asunder all who come within his reach. And
his followers range themselves near him; in their last
day's work they take such good vengeance that they
spare not their strength at all. Alexander's knights
lament that there were no more than thirteen of them
left, though even but now there were twenty-and-
six. Alexander well-nigh raves with fury when he
sees such havoc among his men, who are thus killed
and wounded; but he is not slow to revenge. He has
found at hand by his side a long and heavy beam,
and goes to strike therewith a traitor, and neither the
foeman's shield nor hauberk availed him a whit
against being borne to the ground. After him he
attacks the count; in order to strike well he raises
the beam, and he deals him such a blow with his
square-hewn beam that the axe falls from his hands,
and he was so stunned and so weak that if he had not

leaned against the wall his feet would not have sup-
ported him.

With this blow the battle ceases. Alexander leaps
towards the count, and seizes him in such wise that
he cannot move. No need is there to tell more of
the others, for easily were they vanquished when they
saw their lord taken. They capture them all, with
the count, and lead them away in dire shame, even
as they had deserved. Of all this King Arthur's host,
who were without, knew not a word; but in the
morning, when the battle was ended, they had found
their shields among the bodies; and the Greeks
were raising a very loud lamentation for their lord—
but wrongly. On account of his shield which they
recognise, they one and all make great mourning,
and swoon over his shield, and say that they have lived
too long. Cornix and Nerius swoon, and when they
come to themselves they blame their lives for being
yet whole in them. And so do Torins and Acori-
ondes; the tears ran in streams from their eyes right
on to their breasts. Life and joy are but vexation
to them. And above all Parmenides has dishevelled
and torn his hair. These five make so great a mourn-
ing for their lord that greater there cannot be. But
they disquiet themselves in vain; instead of him they
are bearing away another, and yet they think that

they are bearing away their lord.   The other shields
too, cause them much sorrow, by reason whereof they
think that the bodies are those of their comrades ; and
they swoon and lament over them.   But the shields
lie one and all, for of their men there was but
one slain, who was named Neriolis.   Him truly
would they have borne away, had they known the
truth.   But they are in as great distress about the
others as about him, and they have borne and taken
them all.   About all but one they are mistaken, but
even like a man who dreams, who believes a lie instead
of truth, the shields made them believe that this
lie was true.   They are deceived by the shields.
They have set out with the bodies of the slain, and
have come to their tents, where there were many
folk lamenting, but one and all of the others joined
in the lament the Greeks were making.   There was
a great rally to their mourning.   Now Soredamors,
who hears the wailing and the lament for her friend,
thinks and believes that she was born in an evil hour.
For anguish and grief she loses memory and colour,
and this it is that grieves and wounds her much—
that she dare not openly show her grief : she has
hidden her mourning in her heart.   And yet if any
one had marked it, he would have seen by her counte-
nance and by her outer semblance that she suffered

great pain and sorrow of body; but each one had enough to do to utter his own grief, and recked nought of another's. Each was lamenting his own sorrow, for they find their kinsmen and their friends in evil case, for the river-bank was covered with them. Each lamented his own loss, which is heavy and bitter. There the son weeps for the father, and here the father for the son; this man is swooning over his cousin, and this other over his nephew; thus in each place they lament fathers and brothers and kinsmen. But conspicuous above all is the lament that the Greeks were making, although they might with justice expect great joy; for the greatest mourning of all the host will soon turn to joy.

The Greeks are raising great lamentation without, and those who are within are at great pains how to let them hear that whereof they will have much joy. They disarm and bind their prisoners, who beg and pray them to take now their heads; but the king's men do not will or deign to do this. Rather they say that they will keep them until they deliver them to the king, who then will give them their due, so that their merits will be requited. When they had disarmed them all, they have made them mount the battlements, in order to show them to their folk below. Much does this kindness displease them; since they

saw their lord taken and bound, they were not a whit
glad.  Alexander from the wall above swears by God
and the saints of the world that never will he let a
single one of them live, but will kill them all, and none
shall stay his hand, if they do not all go to yield
themselves up to the king before he can take them.
" Go," quoth he, " I bid you, to my lord without
fail and place yourselves at his mercy.  None of you
save the count here has deserved death.  Never shall
ye lose limb or life if ye place yourselves at his mercy.
If ye do not redeem yourselves from death merely
by crying ' Mercy,' very little confidence can ye
have in your lives or in your bodies.  Issue forth all
disarmed to meet my lord the king, and tell him
from me that Alexander sends you.  Ye will not
lose your pains, for the king my lord will remit for
you all his wrath and indignation, so gentle and
debonair is he.  And if ye will to do otherwise,
ye will have to die, for never will pity for you seize
him."  All of them together believe this counsel;
they do not stop till they reach the king's tent, and
they have all fallen at his feet.  Now is it known
throughout the host what they have told and related.
The king mounts, and all have mounted with him,
and they come spurring to the castle, for no longer
do they delay.

Alexander issues forth from the castle towards the
king, to whom his sight was well pleasing, and he has
yielded up to him the count. And the king has no
longer delayed to do justice on him immediately;
but he greatly praises and extols Alexander, and all
the rest greet him with ceremony, and praise and
extol him loudly. There is none who does not
manifest joy. The mourning that they were formerly
making yields to joy; but no joy can be compared
with that of the Greeks. The king bids them give
him the cup, which was very magnificent and worth
fifteen marks, and he tells and assures him that there
is nought, however dear, save the crown and the
queen, that he will not yield to him if he will to ask
it. Alexander dares not utter his desire in this
matter, yet knows well that the king would not dis-
appoint him if he asked for his lady-love; but he
greatly fears that he might displease her, who would
have had great joy thereat, for rather does he wish
grief for himself without her than to have her without
her will. Therefore he begs and requests a respite,
for he does not wish to make his request till he know
her pleasure in the matter; but he has sought neither
respite nor delay in possessing himself of the golden
cup. He takes the cup, and generously entreats my
Lord Gawain until he accepts this cup from him;

but with exceeding great reluctance has that knight
accepted it. When Soredamors has heard the true
news anent Alexander, much did it please and delight
her. When she knew that he is alive, she has such
joy thereof that it seems to her that never can she
have grief for an hour; but too long, as it seems
to her, does he tarry to come as he is wont. Soon
she will have what she desires, for the two vie with
each other in their yearning for the same thing.

Alexander greatly longed to be able to feast his
eyes on her, if only with one sweet look. Already
for a long time would he fain have come to the
queen's tent, if he had not been kept elsewhere.
Delay displeased him much; so soon as ever he could,
he came to the queen in her tent. The queen has
met him, for she knew much of his thought without
his ever having spoken, but well had she perceived it.
As he enters the tent she salutes him, and takes pains
to greet him with due ceremony; well she knows
what occasion brings him. Because she wishes to
serve him to his liking, she puts Soredamors by his
side, and they three were alone conversing, far from
the others. The queen is the first to begin, for she
had no doubt at all that they loved each other, he
her and she him. Well she thinks to know it for a
certainty, and is convinced that Soredamors could

not have a better lover. She was seated between them, and begins a discourse which came aptly and in season.

"Alexander," quoth the queen, "love is worse than hatred, for it grieves and bewilders its devotee. Lovers know not what they do, when the one hides his feelings from the other. In love there is much grievous toil : he who does not make a bold beginning in the laying of the foundation can scarce put on the coping-stone. The saying goes that there is nothing so difficult to cross as the threshold. I wish to instruct you about love, for well I know that love is using you badly. For this reason have I taken you to task, and take care that you conceal nought of it from me, for clearly have I seen from the countenances of each that of two hearts you have made one. Never seek to hide it from me. You act very foolishly in that the twain of you tell not your thoughts, for you are killing each other by this concealment ; you will be Love's murderers. Now I counsel you that you seek not to satisfy your love by rape or by lust. Unite yourselves in honourable marriage. Thus, as it seems to me, your love will last long. I venture to assure you of this, that if you have a mind for it, I will bring about the marriage."

When the queen had disburdened her heart, Alex-

ander on his side disclosed his. " Lady," quoth he,
" I deny nought whereof you charge me, rather do I
quite admit all that you say. Never do I seek to
be free from love, so as not always to devote myself
to it. This that you of your pity have told me
greatly pleases and delights me. Since you know my
will, I know not why I should any longer conceal it
from you. Very long ago, if I had dared, I would
have confessed it, for the concealment has pained
me much. But perhaps this maiden would in no
wise will that I should be hers and she mine. If
she grants me nought of herself, yet still I give myself
to her." At these words she trembled, and she
does not refuse this gift. She betrays the wish of
her heart both in words and looks ; for trembling
she gives herself to him, and says that never will
she make any reservation of will or heart or person,
but will be wholly at the queen's command and will
do all her pleasure. The queen embraces them both,
and gives the one to the other. Laughing, she says :
" I yield to thee, Alexander, the body of thy love.
Well I know that thou art not alarmed thereat.
Let who will look askance thereat, I give you the one
to the other. Hold thou what is thine, and thou,
Alexander, what is thine." She has what is hers,
and he what is his ; he all of her, and she all of him.

The betrothal took place that very day, at Windsor without a doubt, with the consent and permission of my Lord Gawain and the king. None could tell, I ween, of the magnificence and feasting, of the joy and pleasaunce so great that at the wedding there would not have been more. But inasmuch as it would displease most people, I will not waste or spend one word thereon, for I wish to apply myself to the telling of something better.

On one day at Windsor had Alexander so much honour and joy as pleased him. Three joys and three honours he had. One was for the castle that he took; the second for that King Arthur promised that he would give him, when the war was ended, the best realm in Wales: that day Arthur made him king in his halls. The greatest joy was the third, because his lady-love was queen of the chessboard whereof he was king. Before five months were passed, Soredamors was great with human seed and grain, and she bore it till her time. Such was the seed in its germ that the fruit came according to its kind. A fairer child there could not be before or after. They called the child Cligés.

Born was Cligés, in memory of whom this story was put into French. Ye shall hear me tell fully and relate of him and of his knightly service when he

shall have come to such an age that he will be destined
to grow in fame. But meanwhile it happened in
Greece that the emperor who ruled Constantinople
came to his end. He was dead; he needs must die,
for he could not pass the term appointed. But
before his death he assembled all the high barons of
his land, in order to send and fetch Alexander his
son, who was in Britain, where right willingly he
tarried. The messengers depart from Greece; o'er
the sea they take their voyage, and there a tempest
overtakes them which sorely distresses their ship and
their folk. They were all drowned in the sea save
one treacherous fellow, a renegade, who loved Alis
the younger son more than Alexander the elder.
When he had escaped from the sea, he has returned
to Greece and related that they had all been drowned
in a storm on the sea when they were returning from
Britain and were bringing away their lord; not one
of them had escaped save he only from the storm and
the peril. His lying tale was believed. Unopposed
and unchallenged they take Alis and crown him: they
give to him the empire of Greece. But it was not
long ere Alexander knew for a certainty that Alis
was emperor. Forthwith he has taken leave of King
Arthur, for by no means will he resign his land to
his brother without a fight. The king in no wise

deters him from the plan; rather he bids him lead
away with him so great a multitude of Welsh, Scots,
and Cornishmen that his brother will not dare to
stand his ground when he shall see the host assembled.
Alexander might have led away a great force, had he
willed. But he has no care to destroy his people,
if his brother will answer him in such wise as to per-
form his promise. He led away forty knights, and
Soredamors and his son. These two would he not
leave behind, for they were meet to be greatly loved.
They sailed from Shoreham, where they took leave of
the whole court; they had fair winds, the ship ran
much more swiftly than a fleeing stag. Before the
month had passed, I ween, they came to anchor
before Athens, a city very magnificent and strong.
The emperor, in sooth, was staying in the city, and
there was a great gathering there of the high barons
of the land. As soon as they were arrived, Alexander
sends a trusted servant into the city to know if he
could have a fitting welcome there, or if they will
deny that he is their rightful lord.

The bearer of this message was a courteous and
prudent knight whom men called Acorionde, a man
of wealth and eloquence, and he was much esteemed
in the land, for he was a native of Athens. From of
old his forbears had always had very high lordship in

the city. When he had heard told that the emperor
was in the city, he goes to contend with him for
the crown on behalf of Alexander his brother, and
he cannot pardon him for that he has kept it un-
justly. Straight into the palace has he come, and
finds many a one who greets him fair; but he gives
no answer, nor does he say a word to any man who
greets him, rather he waits until he may hear what
will and what mind they have toward their true lord.
He does not stop till he reaches the emperor; he
greets him not, nor bows to him, nor calls him em-
peror. "Alis," quoth he, "I bear thee a message
from Alexander, who is out yonder in this harbour.
Hear what word thy brother sends to thee: he asks
of thee what is his, and seeks nought that is contrary
to justice. Constantinople, which thou holdest, ought
to be his, and will be his. Neither reasonable nor
right would it be that there should be discord 'twixt
you twain. Take my counsel, and come to terms with
him, and give him the crown in peace, for it is right
meet that thou yield it to him."

Alis replies: "Fair sweet friend, thou hast taken
on thyself a foolish errand in that thou hast brought
this message. No comfort hast thou brought to me,
for I know well that my brother is dead. It would
be a great consolation to me if he were alive and I

knew it. Never will I believe it till I see him. He is dead a while ago, and that is a grief to me. Not a word that thou sayest do I believe. And if he is alive, wherefore comes he not? Never need he fear that I will not give him land in plenty. He is mad if he keeps aloof from me, and if he serve me he will never be the worse for it. Never will there be any man that will hold the crown and the empire against me." Acorionde hears that the emperor's reply is not favourable, but by no fear is he withheld from speaking his mind. "Alis," quoth he, "may God confound me if the matter is left thus. On thy brother's behalf I defy thee, and on his behoof, as is meet, I exhort all those that I see here to leave thee and come over to his side. It is meet that they cleave to him; him ought they to make their lord. He who is loyal, let now his loyalty appear."

With this word he leaves the court, and the emperor on his side summons those in whom he most trusts. From them he seeks counsel as to his brother who thus challenges him, and seeks to know if he can fully trust them not to give support or aid to him in this attack. Thus he hopes to prove each one, but he finds not even one to cleave to him with regard to the war; rather do they bid him remember the war that Eteocles waged against Polynices, who was his

own brother, in which the one killed the other with
his own hands.    " A like thing may chance with
regard to you if you are bent on pursuing war, and
the land will be ruined by reason thereof."  Therefore
they counsel him to seek such a peace as may be
reasonable and honourable, and that the one make
no unreasonable demands on the other.   Now Alis
hears that if he does not make a fair covenant with
his brother, all the barons will desert him, and he
said they will never desire an arrangement which
he cannot equitably make; but he establishes in the
covenant that, whate'er the outcome of the matter,
the crown remain to him.

In order to make firm and lasting peace, Alis sends
one of his masters-at-arms and bids Alexander come
to him and rule all the land, but that he do Alis so
much honour as to allow him to keep the name of
emperor and let him have the crown; thus if he will
can this covenant be made 'twixt the twain of them.
When this thing was related and told to Alexander,
his folk have mounted with him and have come to
Athens.   With joy were they received; but it does
not please Alexander that his brother should have
the lordship of the empire and of the crown, if he
give him not his promise that never will he wed woman,
but that after him Cligés shall be emperor of Con-

stantinople. Thus are the brothers reconciled.
Alexander makes him swear, and Alis grants and war-
rants him, that never as long as he shall live will he
take wife. They are reconciled and remain friends.
The barons manifest great joy; they take Alis for
emperor, but before Alexander come affairs great
and small. Whatever he commands and says is done,
and little is done except through him. Alis has no
longer anything but the name—for he is called
emperor—but Alexander is served and loved, and he
who does not serve him through love must needs
do so through fear. By means of love and fear he
rules all the land according to his will. But he
whose name is Death spares no man, weak or strong,
but slays and kills them all. Alexander was destined
to die, for a sickness for which there was no remedy
took him in its grip; but before death came upon
him he sent for his son, and said: " Fair son Cligés,
never canst thou know how much prowess and valour
thou shalt have if thou go not first to prove thyself
at King Arthur's court on both the Britons and the
French. If fate lead thee thither, so bear and demean
thyself that thou remain unknown till thou hast
proved thyself on the flower of the knighthood
at the court. I counsel thee that thou believe
me in this matter, and that if opportunity comes

thou fear not to put thy fortune to the test with
thy uncle, my Lord Gawain. Prithee forget not
this."

After this exhortation he lived not long. Sore-
damors had such grief thereat that she could not live
after him. For sheer grief she died when he died.
Alis and Cligés both mourned for them, as they were
bound, but in time they ceased to mourn. For all
mourning must come to an end; all things needs
must cease. Ill is it to prolong mourning, for no
good can come of it. The mourning has ceased, and
for a long time after the emperor has refrained from
taking wife, for he would fain strive after loyalty.
But there is no court in all the world that is pure
from evil counsel. Nobles often leave the right
way through the evil counsels to which they give
credence, so that they do not keep loyalty. Often
do his men come to the emperor, and they give him
counsel, and exhort him to take a wife. So much
do they exhort and urge him, and each day do they
so much beset him, that through their great impor-
tunity they have turned him from his loyalty, and
he promises to do their will. But he says that she
who is to be lady of Constantinople must needs
be very graceful and fair and wise, rich and of high
degree. Then his counsellors say to him that they

will make ready, and will hie them into the German
land to sue for the daughter of the emperor. They
counsel him to take her, for the emperor of Germany
is very mighty and very powerful, and his daughter is
so fair that never in Christendom was there a damsel
of such beauty. The emperor grants them all their
suit, and they set out on the way like folk well equipped.
They have ridden in their days' journeys until they
found the emperor at Ratisbon, and asked him to
give his elder daughter for their lord's behoof.

The emperor was full blithe at this embassy, and
gladly has he promised them his daughter, for he in
no wise abases himself by so doing, and abates not
one jot of his dignity. But he says that he had
promised to give her to the Duke of Saxony, and that
the Greeks could not take her away unless the em-
peror came and brought a mighty force, so that the
duke could not do him hurt or injury on the way
back to Greece.

When the messengers had heard the emperor's
reply, they take their leave and set out once more for
home. They have returned to their lord, and have
told him the reply. And the emperor has taken
chosen men, knights proven in arms, the best that
he has found, and he takes with him his nephew, for
whose sake he had vowed that he would never take

wife as long as he lived.   But in no wise will he keep
this vow if he can win to reach Cologne.   On a day
appointed he departs from Greece and shapes his
course towards Germany, for he will not fail, for
blame nor for reproach, to take a wife.   But his
honour will wane thereby.   He does not stop till he
reaches Cologne, where the emperor had established
his court for a festival held for all Germany.   When
the company of the Greeks had come to Cologne,
there were so many Greeks and so many Germans
from the north that more than sixty thousand had
to find quarters outside the town.

Great was the gathering of folk, and very great
was the joy that the two emperors showed, for they
were right glad to meet face to face.   In the palace,
which was very long, was the assembly of the barons ;
and now the emperor sent for his beautiful daughter.
The maiden did not tarry.   Straightway she came
into the palace ; and she was fair and so well shaped,
just as God Himself had made her, for it pleased Him
greatly to show such workmanship as to make people
marvel.   Never did God, who fashioned her, give
to man a word that could express so much beauty
that there was not in her still more beauty.

Fenice was the maiden named, and not without
reason ; for just as the bird Phœnix is fairest above

all others, and there cannot be more than one phœnix at a time, so Fenice, I deem, had no peer for beauty. It was a wonder and a marvel, for never again could Nature attain to framing her like. Inasmuch as I should say less than the truth, I will not in words describe arms, nor body, nor head, nor hands; for if I had a thousand years to live, and each day had doubled my wisdom, I should still waste all my time and yet never express the truth of it. I know well that, if I meddled with it, I should exhaust all my wisdom upon it, and should squander all my pains— for it *would* be wasted pains. The maiden has hastened and has come into the palace with head uncovered and face bare, and the sheen of her beauty sheds greater light in the palace than four carbuncles would have done. Now Cligés had doffed his cloak in presence of his uncle, the emperor. The day was somewhat cloudy; but so beauteous were the twain, both the maid and he, that there shot forth from their beauty a ray with which the palace glowed again, just as the sun shines bright and ruddy in the morning.

To describe the beauty of Cligés, I will limn you a portrait, the traits of which shall be very briefly told. He was in the flower of his youth, for he was about fifteen years old. He was fairer and more comely

than Narcissus, who saw his own reflection in the
fountain beneath the elm, and loved it so much,
when he saw it, that he died—so folk say—because
he could not have it.   Much beauty had he and little
wit; but Cligés had greater store of both, just as
fine gold surpasses copper, and yet more than I can
say.   His hair seemed like fine gold, and his face a
fresh-blown rose.   His nose was well shaped and his
mouth beautiful, and he was of great stature as Nature
best knew how to frame him, for in him alone she
put all at once what she is wont to dole out to each
in portions.   In framing him Nature was so lavish
that she put everything into him all at once, and gave
him whatsoever she could.   Such was Cligés, who
had in him wisdom and beauty, generosity and
strength.   He had the timber together with the bark,
and knew more of fencing and of archery, of birds
and of hounds, than Tristram, King Mark's nephew;
not one grace was lacking to Cligés.

   Cligés in all his beauty was standing before his
uncle, and those who did not know him were in a
fever to see him, and also those who do not know the
maiden are eagerly straining to see her; all look at her
with wonder, but Cligés in love directs his eyes to
her secretly, and withdraws them so prudently that
neither in the going or the coming of the gaze can one

consider him a fool for his action. Right lovingly
he regards her; but he does not pay heed to the fact
that the maiden pays him back in kind. In true love,
not in flattery, he gives his eyes into her keeping and
receives hers. Right good seems this exchange to
her, and it would have seemed to her far better if
she had known somewhat of his worth. But she
knows no more than that she sees him fair, and if
she were ever destined to love aught, because of the
beauty that she might see in it, it is not meet that
she should set her heart elsewhere. She has set her
eyes and her heart there, and he, in his turn, has
promised her his. Promised? Nay, but given for
good and all. Given? Nay, i'faith, I lie; he has
not, for no one can give his heart. Needs must I
say it in a different fashion. I will not speak as they
speak who join two hearts in one body; for it is
not true, and has not even the semblance of truth, to
say that one body can have two hearts at once. And
even if they could come together, such a thing could
not be believed. But an it please you to hearken to
me, I shall be able well to render you the reason why
two hearts blend in one without coming together.
In so far only they blend in one that the will of each
passes from one to the other, and the twain have the
same desire; and because they have the same desire,

there are folk who are wont to say that each of them possesses both the hearts. But one heart is not in two places. Well may their desire be the same, and yet each always his own heart, just as many different men can sing in harmony one song or verse; and I prove to you by this parable that one body cannot have two hearts, because one knows the other's will, or because the second knows what the first loves and what he hates. A body cannot have more than one heart any more than the voices which sing in harmony, so that they seem to be but a single voice, can be the voice of one person alone. But it profits me not to dwell on this, for another task demands my care. Henceforth I must speak of the maiden and of Cligés, and ye shall hear of the Duke of Saxony, who has sent to Cologne a nephew of his, a mere stripling, who discloses to the emperor what his uncle, the duke, bids him deliver—that the emperor expect not from him truce or peace if he send not to him his daughter, and let not that man feel confident on the way who thinks to take her thence with him, for he will not find the way void of foes, rather will it be right well defended against him, if she is not given up to the duke.

Well did the stripling deliver his message, all without pride and without presumption; but he finds none, nor knight nor emperor, to reply to him. When he saw that they were all silent, and that they did it from contempt, he is for quitting the court defiantly. But youth and audacity made him challenge Cligés to joust against him ere he departed. They mount to horse in order to tilt; on both sides they count three hundred, so were equal in number. The whole palace is empty and deserted, for there remains there neither man nor woman, nor knight nor damsel, who does not go and mount on the palace roof, on to the battlements, and to the windows, to see and behold those who were to tilt. Even the princess has mounted thither, she whom love had conquered and won to his will. She is seated at a window where she greatly delights to sit, because from thence she can see him whom she has hidden in her heart; nor hath she desire to take him away from that hiding-place, for never will she love any save him. But she knows not what is his name, nor who he is or of what race, nor does it become her to ask, and yet she longs to hear aught whereat her heart may rejoice. Through the window she looks out on the shields where the gold shines, and on those who carry them slung round their necks, and who take delight in the jousting; but her thought and her glance she has wholly set in one direction, for she gives no thought to aught

else. She is eager to gaze on Cligés, and follows him
with her eyes wherever he goes. And he, on his part,
tilts strenuously for her before the eyes of all, only
that she may hear that he is valiant and very skilful ;
for in any case it would be meet that she should
esteem him for his prowess. He turns himself to-
wards the nephew of the duke, who rode apace, break-
ing many lances and discomfiting the Greeks ; but
Cligés, who is mightily vexed thereat, presses with
all his weight on his stirrups, and rides to strike him
so rapidly that the Saxon in spite of himself has
voided his saddle-bows. There was a great stir as
he rose again. The stripling rises and mounts, and
thinks to avenge thoroughly his shame ; but many
a man thinks to avenge his shame, if he is permitted,
who increases it. The youth rushes towards Cligés,
and Cligés lowers his lance to meet him, and attacks
him with such violence that he bears him once more
to the ground. Now has the youth redoubled his
shame, and all his folk are dismayed thereat, for well
they see that never will they leave the fray with
honour, for none of them is there so valiant that, if
Cligés comes attacking him, he can remain in his
saddle-bow to meet him. Right glad thereof are
they of Germany and they of Greece when they see
that their side are sending the Saxons about their

business ; for the Saxons depart as though discomfited,
while the others pursue them with contumely until
they catch them up at a stream. Many of the foe
do they plunge and immerse therein. Cligés, in the
deepest part of the ford, has thrown the duke's nephew,
and so many others with him, that to their shame and
their vexation they flee mournful and sad. But
Cligés returns with joy, bearing off the prize for valour
on both sides ; and he came straight to a door which
was close to the place where Fenice was standing,
who exacts the toll of a sweet look as he enters the
door—a toll which he pays her, for their eyes have
met. Thus has one conquered the other.

But there is no German, whether of the north or
of the south, so much as able to speak, who does not
say, " God ! who is this in whom so great beauty
blooms ?  God ! whence has the power come to
him so early that he has won so great distinction ? "
Thus asks this man and that, " Who is this youth,
who is he ? " till throughout the city they soon
know the truth of it, both his name and his father's,
and the promise which the emperor had made and
granted to him.  It is already so much told and noised
abroad, that even the maiden hears tell of it, who
had great joy in her heart thereat, because now she
can never say that Love has scorned her, nor can she

complain of aught, for he makes her love the fairest,
the most courteous, and the most valiant man that
one could ever find anywhere; but she must needs
have as her husband one who cannot please her, and
she is full of anguish and distress thereat, for she does
not know with whom to take counsel concerning him
whom she desires save only with her own thoughts
as she lies awake. And thought and wakefulness so
deal with her that they blanch her and altogether
change her complexion, so that one can see quite
clearly by her loss of colour that she has not what
she desires, for she plays less than her wont, and
laughs less, and disports herself less; but she hides
it well, and denies it stoutly if any ask what ails her.
Her nurse, who had brought her up from infancy,
was named Thessala, and was versed in the black
art. She was called Thessala, because she was born
in Thessaly, where sorceries are made, taught, and
practised; for the women who are of that country
make charms and enchantments.

Thessala sees that she whom Love has in his power
is wan and pale, and she has addressed her secretly.
" God ! " quoth she, " are you enchanted, my sweet
lady dear, that you have so wan a countenance ?
Much do I wonder what ails you. Tell me, if you
know, in what part this sickness possesses you most;

for if any one can cure you of it, you can rely on me, for well can I give you back your health. Well know I how to cure a man of dropsy, and I know how to cure of gout, of quinsy, and of asthma ; I know so much about the water and so much about the pulse that evil would be the hour in which you would take another leech. And I know, if I dared say it, of enchantments and of charms well proven and true, more than ever Medea knew. Never spake I a word of it to you, and yet I have brought you up till now ; but never reproach yourself at all for it, for never would I have said aught to you if I had not seen for a surety that such a malady has attacked you that you have need of my aid. Lady, tell me your malady, and you will act wisely in doing so before it gets further hold of you. The emperor has set me in charge of you, that I may take care of you, and I have given such diligence that I have kept you in sound health. Now shall I have lost my pains if I heal you not of this ill. Beware that you hide it not from me, be it illness or aught else." The maiden dares not openly disclose her whole desire, because she is greatly afeard that Thessala may blame and dissuade her. And yet because she hears her greatly vaunt and extol herself and say that she is learned in enchantment, in charms and potions, she will tell her what is her case, why her face is pale and wan ; but beforehand she will make her promise that she will hide it for ever and will never dissuade her.

"Nurse," quoth she, "of a truth I thought that I felt no ill, but I shall speedily think that I am sick. The mere fact of my thinking of it causes me much ill and eke alarms me. But how does one know, unless he put it to the test, what may be good and what ill ? My ill differs from all other ills, for—an I be willing to tell you the truth of it—much it joys me and much it grieves me, and I delight in my discomfort ; and if there can be a disease which gives pleasure, my sorrow is my desire and my grief is my health. I know not then whereof I should complain ; for I know nought whence evil may come to me, if it come not from my desire. Possibly my desire is a malady, but I take so much pleasure in that desire that it causes me a pleasant grief, and I have so much joy in my sorrow that my malady is a pleasant one. Thessala, nurse ! tell me now, is not this sorrow, which seems sweet to me and yet which tortures me, a deceitful one ? I know not how I may recognise whether it be an infirmity or no. Nurse ! tell me now the name and the manner and the nature of it. But be well assured that I have no care to recover in any wise, for I cherish the anguish of it exceedingly." Thes-

sala, who was right wise as regards Love and all his
ways, knows and understands by her speech that that
which distracts her proceeds from love; because
she calls and names it sweet, it is certain that she
loves, for all other ills are bitter, save that alone
which comes from loving; but love transmutes its
own bitterness into pleasure and sweetness, and
often turns to its opposite. But Thessala, who
well knew the matter, replies to her: " Fear nought,
I will tell you well both the nature and the name of
your disease. You have told me, methinks, that the
pain which you feel seems to you to be joy and
health: of such a nature is love-sickness, for there
is in it joy and sweetness. Therefore I prove to you
that you love, for I find pleasure in no sickness save
only in love-sickness. All other ills, as a rule, are
always grievous and horrible, but love is pleasant
and tranquil. You love; I am fully certain of it.
I regard it not as base in you, but I will hold it base-
ness if through childishness or folly you conceal your
heart from me." " Nurse, truly you are talking to
no purpose; for first I mean to be certain and sure
that never by any chance will you speak thereof to
any living creature." " Lady, certainly the winds
will speak of it sooner than I, unless you give me per-
mission; and of this I will make you sure—that I will

help you with regard to this matter, so that you may know of a surety that by me you will have your joy." " Nurse, in that case you would have cured me ; but the emperor is giving me in marriage, whereat I am grievously afflicted and sad, because he who pleases me is nephew of him whom I am to wed. And if this man have his joy of me, then have I lost mine, and there is no more joy to be looked for. Rather would I be torn limb from limb than that the love of Iseult and of Tristram should be renewed in the case of us twain, for of them are such mad actions told that I am ashamed to recount them. I could not reconcile myself to the life that Iseult led. Love in her became exceeding base ; for her body belonged to two masters, and her heart entirely to one. Thus she spent her whole life, for she never refused the two. Reason was there none in this love ; but mine is ever constant, and at no cost will a partition ever be made of my body or of my heart. Never of a truth shall my body be debased ; never shall there be two partners of it. Let him who owns the heart have the body also ; he excludes all others from it. But this I cannot know—how he, to whom my heart yields itself, can have my body, since my father is giving me to another, and I dare not gainsay him. And when he shall be lord of my body, if he do aught with it that I do not

wish, it is not meet that it welcome another. More-
over, this man cannot wed wife without breaking
faith; but if he wrong not his nephew, Cligés will
have the empire after his death. But if you can
contrive by your arts that this man, to whom I am
given and pledged, might never have part or lot in
me, you would have done me good service according
to my will. Nurse, prithee strive that this man break
not his faith; for he gave his pledge to the father
of Cligés, promising, just as Alexander had made him
swear, that never would he take wedded wife. His
pledge is about to be broken, for straightway he intends
to wed me. But I cherish Cligés so dearly that I
would rather be buried than that he should lose through
me a farthing of the inheritance which ought to be
his. May never child be born of me by whom he
may be disinherited! Nurse, now bestir yourself in
the matter, that I may be yours for ever." Then
her nurse tells her and assures her that she will weave
such spells and potions and enchantments that she
would be ill-advised to have concern or fear for this
emperor, so soon as he shall have drunk of the potion
that she will give him to drink; and they will both
lie together, but however close she will be to him,
she can be as secure as if there were a wall between
the two of them. "But let not this, and this only,

vex you, if he has his pleasure of you in dreams; for
when he shall be sound asleep, he will have joy of you
in dreaming, and will quite surely think that he has
his joy of you waking, nor will he imagine that it is
a dream or vision or falsehood. He will delight in
you so that he will think he is awake while he is
sleeping."

The maiden loves and approves and esteems this
boon and this service. Her nurse, who promises her
this, and vows to keep faith with her, puts her in
good hope; for by this means she will think to come
to her joy, however long she have to wait. For never
will Cligés be so ill-disposed to her—if he knows that
she loves him, and for his sake lives so as to guard her
maidenhead in order to shield for him his inheritance
—as not to have some pity on her, if he prove himself
of a noble stock, and if he is such as he ought to be.
The maiden believes her nurse, and trusts and con-
fides in her greatly. The one vows and swears to the
other that this plan will be kept so secret that never
will it be known in the future. Thus the parley is
ended; and when it came to the morning, the
emperor of Germany sends for his daughter. She
comes at his command—but why should I spin out
my story? The two emperors together have so
arranged matters that the marriage takes place,

and joy begins in the palace. But I will not delay
to speak of each thing severally. I will turn my tale
to Thessala, who does not cease to make and mix
potions.

Thessala crushes her potion, she puts therein spices
in plenty for sweetening and blending. Well does
she pound and mix it, and strains it till the whole is
clear, and there is nought acid or bitter there; for
the spices which are in it make it sweet and of pleasant
odour. When the potion was prepared, then had
the day run its course, and the tables were placed for
supper and the tablecloths laid; but she delays the
supper. It is Thessala's task to spy out by what
device, by what messenger, she will send her potion.
They were all seated at the banquet, they had had
more than six courses, and Cligés was serving his uncle.
Thessala, who sees him serve, reflects that he is wasting
his service, for he is serving to his own disinheritance,
and this is a great sorrow and anxiety to her. Then,
like the courteous dame that she is, she bethinks herself
that she will make him, to whom it will be joy and
profit, serve the potion. Thessala sends for Cligés,
and he went straightway to her, and has inquired
and asked of her why she had sent for him. "Friend,"
quoth she, "at this banquet I wish to pay the em-
peror the flattering meed of a potion that he will

greatly esteem. I will not that he drink to-night, either at supper or at bedtime, of any other drink. I think that it will give him much pleasure, for never did he taste of aught so good, nor did any beverage ever cost so much; and take good care—I warn you of this—that no other drink of it, because there is too little of it for that. And, moreover, I give you this advice, that he never know whence it came; but let him think it came by accident, that you found it among the presents, and that because you tested it, and perceived by the scent of its bouquet the fragrance of good spices, and because you saw that it sparkled, you poured the wine into his cup. If by chance he inquire of it, that will doubtless be the end of the matter. But have no evil suspicion anent aught that I have said, for the beverage is pure and wholesome and full of good spices, and it may be, as I think, that at some future time it will make you blithe." When he hears that good will come of it, he takes the potion and goes away, for he knows not that there is aught wrong. In a cup of crystal he has set it before the emperor. The emperor has taken the cup, for he has great trust in his nephew. He drinks a mighty draught of the potion, and now he feels the virtue of it; for it penetrates from the head to the heart, and from the heart it returns to his head, and it permeates him again and again. It saturates his whole body without hurting him. And by the time the tables were removed, the emperor had drunk so much of the beverage, which had pleased him, that never will he get free of it. Each night while asleep he will be intoxicated, and yet it will excite him so much that, though asleep, he will dream that he is awake.

Now is the emperor mocked. Many bishops and abbots there were at the benediction and consecration of the bed. When it was bedtime, the emperor, as it behoved him, lay with his wife that night. " As it behoved him "—therein have I lied ; for he never embraced or touched her, though they lay together in one bed. At first the maiden trembles, for greatly does she fear and feel alarm lest the potion take no effect. But it has so bewitched him that never will he have his will of her or of another save when asleep. But then he will have such ecstasy as one can have in dreaming, and yet he will hold the dream for true. In one word I have told you all : never had he other delight of her than in dreams. Thus must he needs fare evermore, if he can lead his bride away ; but before he can hold her in safety a great disaster, I ween, may befall him. For when he will return home, the duke, to whom she was first given, will be no laggard. The duke has gathered a great force, and has occupied all the marches, and his spies are at the court, and inform him each day of all he wants to know, and tell him all the measures he must take, and how long they will tarry and when they will return, through what places and by what passes. The emperor did not long tarry after the wedding. Blithely he departs from Cologne, and the emperor of Germany escorts him with a very great company, because he greatly fears and dreads the might of the Duke of Saxony.

The two emperors proceed, and stop not till they reach Ratisbon; and on one evening they were lodged by the Danube in the meadow. The Greeks were in their tents in the meadows beside the Black Forest. The Saxons, who were observing them, were encamped opposite them. The duke's nephew was left all alone on a hill to keep a look-out, and see whether, peradventure, he might gain any advantage over those yonder, or wreak any mischief upon them. From his post of vantage he saw Cligés riding with three other striplings, who were taking their pleasure, carrying lances and shields in order to tilt and to disport themselves. Now is the duke's nephew bent on attacking and injuring them if ever he can. With five comrades he sets out, and the

six have posted themselves secretly beside the wood
in a valley, so that the Greeks never saw them till
they issued from the valley, and till the duke's nephew
rushes upon Cligés and strikes him so that he wounds
him a little in the region of the spine. Cligés stoops
and bows his head, so that the lance glances off him ;
nevertheless it wounds him a little.

When Cligés perceives that he is wounded, he has
rushed upon the stripling, and strikes him straightway
with such violence that he thrusts his lance right
through his heart and fells him dead. Then the
Saxons, who fear him mightily, all take to flight and
scatter through the heart of the forest, while Cligés,
who knows not of the ambush, commits a reckless
and foolish act, for he separates himself from his
comrades, and pursues in that direction in which the
duke's force was. And now all the host was preparing
to make an attack on the Greeks. Cligés, all alone,
without aid, pursues them, and the youths, all dis-
mayed because of their lord whom they have lost,
come running into the duke's presence, and weeping
recount to him the evil hap of his nephew. The duke
thinks it no light matter ; by God and all His saints
he swears that never in all his life will he have joy
or good luck as long as he shall know that the slayer of
his nephew is alive. He says that he who will bring

him Cligés' head shall verily be deemed his friend, and will give him great comfort. Then a knight has boasted that the head of Cligés will be offered to the duke by him ; let the duke but rely on him.

Cligés pursues the youths till he swooped down on the Saxons and is seen by the knight who has engaged to carry off his head. Straightway that knight departs and stays no longer. But Cligés has retreated, in order to elude his enemies, and he returned at full gallop thither where he had left his comrades. But he has found none of them there, for they had returned to the tents to relate their adventure. And the emperor summoned Greeks and Germans alike to horse. Through all the host the barons speedily arm themselves and mount. But the Saxon knight, all armed, his visor laced, has continued to pursue Cligés at a gallop. Cligés, who never wished to have aught in common with a recreant or coward, sees him come alone. First of all the knight has assailed him with words : he stoutly calls him baseborn fellow, for he could not conceal the mind he had of him. " Fellow," quoth he, " here wilt thou leave the forfeit for my lord, whom thou hast slain. If I bear not off thy head with me, then esteem me not worth a bad Byzantine coin. I will to make the duke a present of it, for I will not accept any other forfeit in its stead. So much will I render to him for his nephew, and he will have had a good exchange for him." Cligés hears that the Saxon is abusing him as a madman and low-bred fellow. " Man," quoth he, " now defend yourself, for I defy you to take my head, and you shall not have it without my leave." Forthwith the one seeks the other. The Saxon has missed his stroke, and Cligés thrusts so hard that he made man and steed fall all in a heap. The steed falls backwards on his rider with such violence that it completely breaks one of his legs. Cligés dismounts on the green grass and disarms him. When he had disarmed him, then he dons the arms himself, and has cut off his head with the victim's own sword. When he had cut off his head, he has fixed it on to the point of his lance, and says that he will present it to the duke, to whom his enemy had vowed to present Cligés' own head if he could meet him in the fight. No sooner had Cligés placed the helm on his head, taken the shield (not his own, but the shield of him who had fought with him), and no sooner had he mounted on the foeman's horse, leaving his own riderless in order to dismay the Greeks, than he saw more than a hundred banners and battalions, great and fully equipped, of Greeks and Germans mingled. Now will begin a very fierce and cruel mellay between the

Saxons and the Greeks. As soon as Cligés sees them
come, he goes straight towards the Saxons, and the
Greeks exert themselves to pursue him, for on account
of his arms they do not know him; and his uncle,
who sees the head that he is bringing, is marvellously
discomforted thereat. No wonder is it if he fears
for his nephew. The whole host musters in his wake,
and Cligés lets them pursue him, in order to begin
the mellay, till the Saxons perceive him coming, but
the arms with which he is clad and furnished mislead
them all. He has mocked at them and scorned them;
for the duke and all the others, as he advanced with
feutred lance, say: "Our knight is coming! On
the point of the lance that he holds he is bringing the
head of Cligés, and the Greeks follow after him.
Now to horse to succour him!" Then they all
give the rein to their horses, and Cligés spurs towards
the Saxons, covering himself behind his shield and
doubling himself up, his lance upright, the head on
its point. Not one whit less courage than a lion
had he, though he was no stronger than another.
On both sides they believe that he is dead—Saxons,
and Greeks and Germans—and the one side are blithe
thereat, and the other side grieved; but soon will the
truth be known. For now has Cligés no longer held
his peace: shouting, he gallops towards a Saxon, and

strikes him with his ashen lance, with the head on it, full in the breast, so that he has lost his stirrups, and he calls out, " Barons, strike ! I am Cligés, whom you seek. On now, bold freeborn knights ! Let there be no coward, for ours is the first shock. Let no craven taste of such a dainty dish."

The emperor greatly rejoiced when he heard his nephew Cligés who thus addresses and exhorts them ; right glad and comforted is he thereof. And the duke is utterly dumfounded ; for now he knows well that he is betrayed unless his force is the greater ; he bids his men close their ranks and keep together. And the Greeks in close array have not gone far from them ; for now they are spurring and pricking. On both sides they couch their lances and meet and receive each other, as it behoved them to do in such a fight. At the first encounter they pierce shields and shatter lances, cut girths, break stirrups ; the steeds stand bereft of those who fall upon the field. But no matter what the others do, Cligés and the duke meet, they hold their lances couched, and each strikes the other on his shield with so great valour that the lances, which were strong and well wrought, break into splinters. Cligés was a skilful horseman : he remained upright in his saddle, never stumbling nor wavering. The duke has lost his saddle and,

in spite of himself has voided the saddle-bows. Cligés
thinks to take him and lead him away captive, and
mightily toils and strains, but the strength he needed
was not his. For the Saxons were all around, and they
rescue their duke by force. Nevertheless Cligés
leaves the field without injury with a prize, for he
leads away the duke's steed, which was whiter than
wool, and which for the use of a man of valour was
worth all the possessions of Octavian of Rome : the
steed was an Arab one. Great joy manifest Greeks
and Germans when they see Cligés mounted on it,
for they had seen the worth and the perfection of the
Arab ; but they did not suspect an ambush, nor
will they ever perceive it till they receive great loss
therefrom.

A spy has come to the duke, with news at which he
has waxed full joyous. "Duke," quoth the spy,
" no man has been left in all the tents of the Greeks
who can defend himself. Now can thy men take
the daughter of the emperor, if thou wilt trust my
words, while thou seest the Greeks desperately bent
on the fight and on the battle. Give me a hundred
of thy knights and I will give them thy lady-love.
By an old and lonely path I will lead them so prudently
that they shall not be seen or met by Saxon or German,
till they will be able to take the maiden in her tent

and lead her away so unhindered that never will she be denied them." The duke is blithe at this thing. He has sent a hundred and more wise knights with the spy, and the spy has led them in such wise that they take the maiden as a prize, nor have they spent great force thereon, for easily were they able to lead her away. When they had taken her some distance from the tents, they sent her away attended by twelve of them, nor did the rest accompany the twelve far. Twelve of them lead away the maiden, the others have told the duke the news of their success. Nought else was there that the duke had desired, and straightway he makes a truce with the Greeks till the morrow. They have given and accepted a truce. The duke's men have returned, and the Greeks without any delay return each one to his tent. But Cligés remained alone on a hill so that no one noticed him—till he saw the twelve coming and the damsel whom they were taking away at full speed and at a gallop. Cligés, who longs to gain renown, forthwith dashes in their direction; for he thinks to himself, and his heart tells him, that it is not for nothing they are fleeing. The very moment that he saw them he dashes after them, and they see him, but they think and believe a foolish thing. "The duke is following us," each one says,

" let us wait for him a little, for he has left the host unattended and is coming after us very swiftly." There is not a single one who does not believe this. They all desire to go to meet him, but each desires to go alone. Cligés must needs descend into a great valley between two mountains. Never would he have recognised their insignia if they had not come to meet him or if they had not awaited him. Six of them advanced to meet him, but soon will they have had an ill meeting with him. The others stay with the maiden and lead her on gently at a walking pace. And the six go at full speed, spurring incessantly through the valley. He who had the swiftest horse outstripped all the rest, crying aloud : " Duke of Saxony ! God preserve thee ! Duke ! we have regained thy lady. Now shall the Greeks never carry her off, for she will now be given and handed over to thee." When Cligés has heard these words that the other cries out, no smile had he in his heart—rather is it a marvel that frenzy does not seize him. Never was any wild beast, leopardess or tigress or lioness, who sees her young taken, so embittered and furious and lusting for the fight as was Cligés, who cares not to live if he fail his lady. Rather would he die than not have her. Very great wrath has he for this calamity, and exceeding great courage does it give him.

He spurs and pricks the Arab and goes to deal the blazoned shield of the Saxon such a blow that—I lie not—he made him feel the lance at his heart. This has given Cligés confidence. More than a full acre's measure has he spurred and pricked the Arab before the second has drawn near, for they came one by one. The one has no fear for the other, for he fights with each singly and meets them one by one, nor has the one aid of the other. He makes an attack on the second, who thought to tell the supposed duke news of Cligés' discomfiture and to rejoice thereat, as the first had done. But Cligés recks little of words or of listening to his discourse. He proceeds to thrust his lance in his body, so that when he draws it out again the blood gushes out, and he bereaves his foe of life and speech. After the two he joins issue with a third, who thinks to find him over-joyed and to gladden him with news of his own dis-comfiture. He came spurring against him, but before he has the chance to say a word, Cligés has thrust his lance a fathom deep into his body. To the fourth he gives such a blow on the neck that he leaves him in a swoon on the field. After the fourth he gallops against the fifth, and then after the fifth against the sixth. Of these none stood his ground against him, rather does Cligés leave them all silent and dumb.

Still less has he feared and more boldly sought the rest of them. After this has he no concern about these six.

When he was free from care as regards these, he goes to make a present of shame and of misfortune to the rest, who are escorting the maiden. He has overtaken them and attacks them like a wolf, who, famished and fasting, rushes on his prey. Now seems it to him that he was born in a good hour, since he can display his chivalry and courage before her who is all his life. Now is he dead if he free her not, and she, on the other hand, is likewise dead, for she is greatly discomforted for him, but does not know that he is so near her. Cligés, with feutred lance, has made a charge which pleased her, and he strikes one Saxon and then another, so that with one single charge he has made them both bite the dust and splinters his ashen lance. The foemen fall in such anguish that they have no power to rise again to hurt or molest him; for they were sore wounded in their bodies. The other four in great wrath go all together to strike Cligés, but he neither stumbles nor trembles, nor have they unhorsed him. Swiftly he snatches from the scabbard his sword of sharpened steel, and that she who awaits his love may be right grateful to him, he encounters with lightning swiftness a Saxon, and

strikes him with his sharp sword, so that he has
severed from his trunk his head and half his neck :
no tenderer pity had he for him. Fenice, who
watches and beholds, knows not that it is Cligés.
Fain would she that it were he ; but because there
is danger, she says to herself that she would not wish
it. For two reasons is she his good friend, for she
fears his death and desires his honour. And Cligés
receives at the sword's point the three who offer him
fierce combat ; they pierce and cleave his shield, but
they cannot get him into their power or cleave the links
of his shirt of mail. And nought that Cligés can reach
stands firm before his blow, for he cleaves and breaks
asunder all ; he wheels round more quickly than the
top which is urged on and driven by the whip.
Prowess and love entwine him and make him bold and
keen in fight. He has dealt so grievously with the
Saxons that he has killed or conquered them all,
wounded some and killed others, but he let one of
them escape, because they were a match one for the
other, and so that by him the duke might know his
loss and mourn. But before this man left him, he
prevailed upon Cligés to tell him his name and went,
for his part, to tell it to the duke, who had great
wrath thereat.

Now the duke hears of his misfortune and had great

grief and great care thereat. And Cligés leads away
Fenice, who thrills and tortures him with the pangs
of love; but if now he does not hear her confession,
long time will love be adverse to him, and also to her,
if she on her side is silent and say not her will; for
now in the hearing one of the other can they reveal
their inmost hearts. But so much do they fear refusal
that they dare not betray their hearts. He fears
that she might reject him, she on her part would have
betrayed herself if she had not feared rejection. And
nevertheless the one betrays his thoughts to the other
with the eyes, if they could only have known it. They
speak by glances with their eyes; but they are so
craven with their tongues that in no wise dare they
speak of the love which masters them. If she dare
not begin it, it is no marvel, for a maiden ought
to be a simple and shy creature. But why does
*he* wait and why does *he* delay, who is thoroughly
bold in her behalf and has shown dread of none but
her? God! whence comes this fear to him that
he fears a single maiden, weak and timid, simple and
shy? At this methinks I see dogs fleeing before the
hare and the fish hunting the beaver, the lamb the
wolf, the dove the eagle. So would it be if the
villein were to flee before his hoe, by which he gains
his livelihood and with which he toils. So would it

be if the falcon were to flee from the duck and the
gerfalcon from the heron, and the great pike from the
minnow, and if the stag were to chase the lion; so
do things go topsy-turvy. But a desire comes upon
me to give some reason why it happens to true lovers
that wit and courage fail them to express what they
have in their thoughts, when they have leisure and
opportunity and time.

You who are being instructed in love, who faith-
fully uphold the customs and rites of his court, and
who never broke his law, whatever might have befallen
you for your obedience, tell me if one can see any-
thing which affords love's delight but that lovers
shiver and grow pale thereat. Never shall there be
a man opposed to me that I do not convince of this,
for he who does not grow pale and shiver thereat,
who does not lose wit and memory, like a thief
pursues and seeks that which is not fittingly his.
A servant who does not fear his lord ought not to
stay in his retinue or serve him. He who does not
esteem his lord does not fear him, and he who does
not esteem him does not hold him dear, but rather
seeks to cheat him and to pilfer somewhat of his
property. For fear ought a servant to tremble
when his lord calls him or sends for him. And he
who commends himself to Love makes Love his

master and his lord, and it is meet that he have him in reverence and greatly fear and honour him, if he wishes to stand well with his court.  Love without fear and without dread is fire without flame and without heat, daylight without sun, honeycomb without honey, summer without flowers, winter without frost, sky without moon, a book without letters.  Thus do I wish to refute such an opponent, for where fear is lacking, there is no love worth mentioning.  It behoves him who wishes to love to fear also, for if he does not, he cannot love; but let him fear her only whom he loves and in her behoof let him be thoroughly bold.  Therefore Cligés commits no fault or wrong if he fears his lady-love.  But for this fear he would not have failed forthwith to have spoken to her of love and sought her love, however the matter had happed, if she had not been his uncle's wife.  For this cause his wound rankles in him and it pains and grieves him the more, because he dare not say what he yearns to say.

Thus they return towards their company, and if they talk of anything, there was in their talk nothing about which they cared.  Each sat on a white horse, and they rode quickly towards the army, where there was great lamentation.  Throughout the host they are beside themselves with grief; but they hit upon an untrue saying when they say that Cligés is dead—thereat is the mourning very great and loud. And they fear for Fenice, they deem not that they will ever have her again; and both for her and for him the whole host is in very great sorrow. But these two will not delay much longer, and the whole state of matters will take a different appearance; for already they have returned to the host and have turned the sorrow into joy. Joy returns and sorrow flies. They all come to meet them, so that the whole host assembles. The two emperors together, when they heard the news about Cligés and about the maiden, go to meet them with very great joy; but each one longs to hear how Cligés had found and rescued the lady. Cligés tells them the tale, and those who hear it marvel greatly thereat and much do they praise his prowess and valour. But, on the other side, the duke is furious, who swears and protests and who declares that, if Cligés dares, there shall be a single combat between the two of them, and that he will order matters in such wise that, if Cligés wins the combat, the emperor shall go away in safety and take the maiden unhindered; but that if he kills or conquers Cligés, who has done him many an injury, let there for this be neither truce nor peace till after each has done his utmost. This the duke

essays, and through an interpreter of his, who knew
Greek and German, gives the two emperors to know
that thus he wishes to have the battle.

The messenger delivers his message in one and the
other language so well that all understood. The
whole host resounds and is in an uproar about it,
and men say that never may it please God that Cligés
fight the battle; and both the emperors are in a very
great alarm thereat; but Cligés falls at their feet and
prays them let it not grieve them, but that, if ever
he has done aught that has pleased them, he may have
this battle as a guerdon and as a reward. And if it
is denied him, never will he for a single day be a
blessing and an honour to his uncle. The emperor,
who held his nephew as dear as duty bade him, with
his hand raises him up from his knees and says: " Fair
nephew, greatly does it grieve me that I know you to
be so wedded to fighting; for after joy I expect sorrow
therefrom. You have made me glad, I cannot deny
it, but much it grieves me to grant this boon and
send you to the battle, for that I see you yet too young.
And I know you to be of such proud courage that in
no wise dare I deny anything that it please you to
ask; for know well that it would be done but to
please you; but if my prayer availed aught, never
would you take on you this burden." " Sire, you are

pleading in vain," quoth Cligés, "for may God confound me if I would accept the whole world on condition that I did not fight this battle. I know not why I should seek from you a long respite or a long delay." The emperor weeps with pity, and Cligés, on his side, weeps with joy when he grants him the battle. There had he wept many a joyful tear, nor had he secured delay nor limit of time: before it was the hour of Prime, by his own messenger was the battle announced to the duke, just as he had demanded it.

The duke, who thinks and believes and imagines that Cligés will not be able to defend himself against him, but that he will soon have slain or conquered him, quickly has himself armed. Cligés, who is longing for the battle, thinks that he need have no care as to how to defend himself against the duke. He asks the emperor for arms and prays him to dub him knight, and of his grace the emperor gives him arms and Cligés takes them, for his heart is enamoured of the battle and much does he desire and long for it. He hastens full swiftly to arm himself: when he was armed from head to foot, the emperor, who was full of anxiety, goes to gird the sword on his side. Cligés mounts on the white Arab fully armed, from his neck he hangs by the straps a shield made of elephant's bone, such that it will neither break nor split, nor had

it blazon or device : the armour was all white, and
the steed and the harness were all whiter than any
snow.

Cligés and the duke are armed, and the one has
announced to the other that they will meet half-way,
and that on both sides their men shall all be without
swords and without lances, bound by oaths and their
word of honour that never as long as the combat shall
last will there be any so bold as to dare to move for any
reason, any more than he would dare to pluck out his
own eye.   Bound by this covenant they have met, and
the delay has seemed very long to each champion, for
each thinks to have the glory and the joy of victory.
But before there was a blow struck, the maiden,
who is much concerned for Cligés, has herself escorted
thither ; but on this is she quite resolved that, if he
dies, she will die.   Never will any hope of consola-
tion avail to deter her from dying with him ; for
without him life has no charm for her.

When all had come into the field, high and low,
young and hoary, and the guards had been set there,
then have both champions taken their lances, and they
meet in no half-hearted way, so that each breaks his
lance and both are unhorsed and fail to keep their
saddles.   But quickly have they risen to their feet,
for they were not at all wounded, and again they

encounter without delay. They play a merry tune
with their swords on the resounding helms, so that
their retinue are amazed, and it seems to those who
watch them that the helmets are on fire and ablaze.
And when the swords rebound, glowing sparks jet
forth as from red-hot iron, which the smith hammers
on the anvil when he draws it from the furnace. Very
lavish are both the warriors in dealing blows in great
store, and each has a good will to pay back quickly
what he borrows; neither the one nor the other ceases
from paying back capital and interest immediately all
without count and without stint. But the duke comes
on in great anger, and right wroth and furious is he
because he has not quelled and slain Cligés at the first
encounter. He deals him a great blow marvellous
and strong, such that at his feet Cligés has fallen
on one knee.

At the blow whereby Cligés fell was the emperor
much amazed, he was no whit less bewildered than if he
had been behind the shield himself. Then Fenice, so
much was she amazed, can no longer restrain herself,
whatever might come of it, from crying: "God!
aid!" as loud as ever she could. But she had called
out but one word when forthwith her voice failed and
she fell swooning and with arms outstretched, so that
her face was a little wounded. Two noble barons

have raised her and have held her on her feet till she
has returned to her senses. But never did any who
saw her, whatever appearance she presented, know why
she swooned. Never did any man blame her for it,
rather they have all praised her; for there is not a
single one who does not believe that she would have
done the same for his sake, if he had been in Cligés'
place; but in all this there is no truth. Cligés,
when Fenice cried, heard and marked her right well.
The sound restored to him strength and courage, and
he springs swiftly to his feet and advanced furiously
to meet the duke, and thrusts at him and presses him
so that the duke was amazed thereat, for he finds him
more greedy for combat, more strong and agile than
he had found him before, it seems to him, when they
first encountered. And because he fears his onset,
he says to him: "Knight, so may God save me,
I see thee right courageous and valiant. But if it
had not been for my nephew, whom I shall never
forget, willingly would I have made peace with thee
and would have released thee from the quarrel, for
never would I have meddled any more in the matter."

"Duke," says Cligés, "what may be your pleasure?
Is it not meet that he who cannot make good his
claim yield it? Of two evils, when one has to choose,
one ought to choose the lesser. When your nephew

picked a quarrel with me, he acted unwisely. I will serve you in the same way, be assured of it, if I ever can, if I do not receive submission from you." The duke, to whom it seems that Cligés was growing in strength every moment, thinks that it is much better for him to stop short half-way before he is altogether wearied out. Nevertheless, he does not confess to him the truth quite openly, but he says: " Knight, I see thee debonair and agile and of great courage. But exceeding young art thou: for this reason I reflect, and I know of a surety that, if I conquer and kill thee, never should I win praise or esteem thereby, nor should I ever see any man of valour in whose hearing I should dare to confess that I had fought with thee; for I should do honour to thee and shame to myself. But if those knowst what honour means, a great honour will it be to thee for ever that thou hast stood thy ground against me even for two encounters only. Now a wish and desire has come to me to release thee from the quarrel and not to fight with thee any longer." " Duke," quoth Cligés, " you talk idly. You shall say it aloud in the hearing of all, and never shall it be told or related that you have done me a kindness or that you have had mercy on me. In the hearing of one and all of these who are here you will have to declare it, if you wish to make peace with me." The duke declares it in the hearing of all. Thus have they made peace and agreement; but whatever the issue of the matter, Cligés had the honour and the renown of it, and the Greeks had very great joy thereof. But the Saxons could not make light of the matter, for well had they all seen their lord exhausted and worsted; nor is there any question but that if he had been able to do better for himself, this peace would never have been made; rather would he have rent the soul out of Cligés' body, if he had been able to do it. The duke returns to Saxony grieved and downcast and ashamed, for of his men there are not two who do not hold him a conquered man, a craven, and a coward. The Saxons, with all their shame, have returned to Saxony. And the Greeks delay no longer; they return towards Constantinople with great joy and with great gladness, for well by his prowess has Cligés assured to them the way. Now the emperor of Germany no further follows or attends them. After taking leave of the Greek folk and of his daughter and of Cligés and of the emperor, he has remained in Germany, and the emperor of the Greeks goes away right glad and right joyful. Cligés, the valiant, the well-bred, thinks of his father's command. If his uncle, the emperor, will grant him leave, he will go to request and pray him to let him go to

Britain to speak to his uncle the king; for he craves
to know and see him. He sets out for the presence
of the emperor, and begs him, if it please him, to let
him go to Britain to see his uncle and his friends.
Very gently has he made this request, but his uncle
refuses it to him when he had heard and listened to
the whole of his request and his story. "Fair
nephew," quoth he, "it pleases me not that you
should wish to leave me. Never will I give you this
leave or this permission without great grief; for right
pleasant and convenient is it that you should be my
partner and co-ruler with me of all my empire."

Now there is nothing which pleases Cligés, since his
uncle denies him what he asks and requests, and he
says: "Fair Sire, it becomes me not, nor am I brave
or wise enough to be given this partnership with
you or with another, so as to rule an empire; very
young am I and know but little. For this reason is
gold applied to the touchstone, because one wishes
to know if it is real gold. So wish I—that is the end
and sum of it—to assay and prove myself where I
think to find the touchstone. In Britain, if I am
valiant, I shall be able to put myself to the touch
with the whetstone and with the true and genuine
assay by which I shall test my prowess. In Britain
are those valiant men of whom honour and prowess

boast. And he who wishes to gain honour ought to join himself to their company, for there the honour resides and is won which appertains to the man of valour. Therefore I ask you this leave, and know of a surety that if you do not send me thither and do not grant me the boon, that I shall go without your leave." "Fair nephew, rather do I give it you freely when I see you thus minded, for I would not have the heart to detain you by force or by prayer. Now may God give you heart and will to return soon, since neither prayer nor prohibition nor force could prevail in the matter. I would have you take with you a talent of gold and of silver, and horses to delight you will I give you all at your choice." No sooner had he said his word than Cligés has bowed to him. All whatsoever the emperor has devised and promised was at once set before him.

Cligés took as much wealth and as many comrades as pleased and behoved him ; but for his own private use he takes away four different steeds, one white, one sorrel, one dun, one black. But I was about to pass over one thing that must not be omitted. Cligés goes to take leave of Fenice, his lady-love, and to ask her leave to depart ; for he would fain commend her to God. He comes before her and kneels down weeping, so that he moistens with his tears all his tunic and his ermine, and he bends his eyes to the ground, for he dares not look straight in front of him, just as if he has committed some wrong and crime towards her, and now shows by his mien that he has shame for it. And Fenice, who beholds him timidly and shyly, knows not what matter brings him, and she has said to him in some distress: "Friend, fair sir, rise; sit by my side, weep no more and tell me your pleasure." "Lady! what shall I say? what conceal? I seek your permission to depart." "Depart? Why?" "Lady! I must go away to Britain." "Tell me then on what quest, before I give you permission." "Lady, my father, when he died and departed this life, prayed me on no account to fail to go to Britain, as soon as I should be a knight. For nothing in the world would I neglect his command. It will behove me not to play the laggard as I go thither. It is a very long journey from here to Greece; and if I were to go thither, the journey from Constantinople to Britain would be very long for me. But it is meet that I take leave of you as being the lady whose I am wholly." Many hidden and secret sighs and sobs had he made on setting out; but no one had eyes so wide open or such good hearing as to be able to perceive for a certainty from hearing or sight that there was love between the twain. Cligés, grievous though it be to him, departs as soon as it is allowed him. He goes away lost in thought, lost in thought remains the emperor and many another, but Fenice is the most pensive of all: she discovers neither bottom nor bound to the thought with which she is filled, so greatly does it overflow and multiply in her. Full of thought she has come to Greece: there was she held in great honour as lady and empress, but her heart and spirit are with Cligés, wherever he turns, nor ever seeks she that her heart may return to her unless he bring it back to her, he who is dying of the malady with which he has slain her. And if he recovers, she will recover; never will he pay dear for it unless she too pay dear. Her malady appears in her complexion, for much has she changed and pale has she grown. The fresh, clear, pure hue that Nature had bestowed has wholly deserted her face. Often she weeps, often sighs: little recks she of her empire and of the wealth she has. She has always in her memory the hour that Cligés departed, the farewell that he took of her, how he changed countenance, how he blanched, his tears and his mien; for he came to weep before her, humble, lowly, and on his knees, as if he must needs worship her. All this is pleasant and sweet for her to recall and to retrace. Then, to provide herself with a luscious

morsel, she takes on her tongue in lieu of spice a
sweet word, and for all Greece she would not wish
that he who said that word should, in the sense
in which she took it, have intended deceit; for
she lives on no other dainty nor does aught else
please her. This word alone sustains and feeds
her and soothes for her all her suffering. She seeks
not to feed herself or quench her thirst with any other
meat or drink; for when it came to the parting,
Cligés said that he was "wholly hers." This word
is so sweet and good to her, that from the tongue it
goes to her heart, and she stores it in her heart as
well as in her mouth, that she may be the surer of
it. She dares not hide this treasure behind any
other lock, and she would never be able to store it
elsewhere so well as in her heart. In no wise will
she ever take it thence, so much she fears thieves and
robbers; but it is without reason that this fear comes
to her, and without reason that she fears birds of prey;
for this possession is immovable; rather is it like
a building which cannot be destroyed by flood or by
fire and which will never move from its place. But
this she knows not, and hence she gives herself agony
and pain to seek out and learn something on which
she can lay hold; for in divers fashions does she
explain it. She holds debate within herself and

makes such replies as these : " With what intention
did Cligés say to me 'I am wholly yours,' if love
did not cause him to say it ? With what power
of mine can I sway him, that he should esteem
me so highly as to make me his lady ?    Is he
not fairer than I, of much nobler birth than I ?    I
see nought but his love that can bestow on me this
gift.  From my own case, for I cannot evade the
scrutiny, I will prove that if he had not loved me he
would never have called himself wholly mine, for
just as I could not be wholly his nor could in honour
say so, if love had not drawn me to him, so Cligés,
on his side, could not in any wise have said that he
was wholly mine, if love has him not in his bonds.    For
if he loves me not, he fears me not.    Love, which gives
me wholly to him, perhaps gives him wholly to me ;
but this thought quite dismays me, that the phrase
is one in common use, and I may easily be deceived,
for many a man there is who in flattery says even to
strangers : ' I am quite at your service, I and whatso-
ever I have.'    And such men are more mocking than
jays.  So I know not what to think ; for it might
well be that thus he spake to flatter me.  But I saw
him change colour and weep right piteously.  To my
mind, his tears, his shamefaced and cast-down counten-
ance, did not come from deceit ; no deceit or trickery

was there there. The eyes, from which I saw the tears fall, did not lie to me. Signs enow could I see there of love, if I know aught of the matter. Yea! I grant that evil was the hour in which I thought it. Evil was the hour that I learnt it and stored it in my heart, for a very great misfortune has happed to me from it. A misfortune? Truly, by my faith! I am dead, since I see not him who has flattered and cajoled me so much that he has robbed me of my heart. Through his deceit and smooth words my heart is quitting its lodging and will not stay with me, so much it hates my dwelling and my manor. Faith! then he who has my heart in his keeping has dealt ill with me. He who robs me and takes away what is mine loves me not, I know it well. I know it? Why then did he weep? Why? It was not for nothing, for he had reason enow. I ought to apply nought of it to myself, because a man's sorrow is very great at parting from those whom he loves and knows. I marvel not that he had grief and sorrow and that he wept when he left his acquaintances. But he who gave him this counsel to go and stay in Britain could have found no better means of wounding me to the heart. One who loses his heart is wounded to the heart. He who deserves sorrow ought to have it, but I never deserved it. Alas!

unhappy that I am! Why then has Cligés slain me
without any fault of mine? But in vain do I re-
proach him; for I have no grounds for this reproach.
Cligés would never never have forsaken me, I know
this well, if his heart had been in like case with mine.
In like case, I think, it is not. And if my heart has
joined itself to his heart, never will it leave it, never
will his go anywhither without mine, for mine follows
him in secret, so close is the comradeship that they
have formed. But, to tell the truth, the two hearts
are very different and contrary. How are they
different and contrary? His is lord and mine is
slave; and the slave, even against his own will, must
do what is for his lord's good, and leave out of sight
all else. But what matters it to me? He cares
nought for my heart or for my service. This division
grieves me much, for thus the one heart is lord
of the two. Why cannot mine all alone avail as
much as his with him? Thus the two would have
been of equal strength. My heart is a prisoner,
for it cannot move unless his moves. And if his
wanders or tarries, mine ever prepares to follow
and go after him. God! why are not our bodies
so near that I could in some way have fetched my
heart back? Have fetched it back? Poor fool!
If I were to take it from where it is lodged so com-

fortably, I might kill it by so doing. Let it stay there. Never do I seek to remove it, rather do I will that it stay with its lord until pity for it come to him; for rather there than here will he be bound to have mercy on his servant, because the two hearts are in a strange land. If my heart knows how to serve up flattery, as one is bound to serve it up at court, it will be rich before it returns. He who wishes to be on good terms with his lord, and to sit beside him on his right, as is now the use and custom, must feign to pluck the feather from his lord's head even when there is no feather there. But here we see an evil trait: when he flatters him to his face and yet his lord has in his heart either baseness or villainy, never will he be so courteous as to tell him the truth, rather he makes him think and believe that no one could be a match for him in prowess or in knowledge, and the lord thinks that the courtier is telling the truth. He who believes another anent some quality which he does not possess knows himself ill; for even if he is faithless and stubborn, base and as cowardly as a hare, niggardly and foolish and malformed, worthless in deeds and in words, yet many a man who mocks at him behind his back extols and praises him to his face; thus then the courtier praises him in his hearing when he speaks of him to another, and yet he pretends that the lord

does not hear what they are speaking about together;
whereas if he really thought that the lord did not
hear, he would never say aught whereat his master
would rejoice. And if his lord wishes to lie, he is
quite ready with his assent, and whatever his lord
says he asserts to be true; never will he who associates
with courts and lords be tongue-tied, his tongue must
serve them with falsehood. My heart must needs do
likewise, if it wishes to have grace of its lord; let it
be a flatterer and cajoler. But Cligés is such a brave
knight, so handsome, so noble, and so loyal that never
will my heart be lying or false, however much it may
praise him, for in him is nothing that can be mended.
Therefore I will that my heart serve him; for the
peasant says in his proverb, 'He who commends
himself to a good man is base if he does not become
better in his service.'" Thus love works on Fenice.
But this torment is delight to her, for she cannot be
wearied by it.

And Cligés has crossed the sea and has come to
Wallingford. There he has demeaned himself in
lordly fashion in a fine lodging at a great cost; but he
thinks ever of Fenice; never does he forget her for an
hour. In the place where he sojourns and tarries,
his retinue, as he had commanded, have inquired and
questioned persistently till they heard told and

related that the barons of King Arthur and the king himself in person had set on foot a tournament in the plains before Oxford, which is near Wallingford. In such wise was the joust arranged that it was to last four days. But Cligés will be able to take time to arm his body, if he lacks anything meanwhile, for there were more than fifteen whole days to the tournament. He speedily sends three of his squires to London, and bids them buy three different sets of armour, one black, another red, the third green, and as they return he bids that each set of arms be covered with new canvas; so that, if anyone meets them on the way, he may not know what will be the hue of the arms which they will bring. The squires now set out, go to London, and find ready all such equipment as they seek. Soon had they finished, soon did they return: they have come back as soon as they could. They show to Cligés the arms that they had brought, and he praises them much. With these that the emperor gave him on the Danube, when he dubbed him knight, he has them stored away and hidden. If anyone now were to ask me why he had them stored away, I would not answer him, for in due time it will be told and related to you, when all the high barons of the land, who will come there to gain fame, will be mounted on their steeds.

On the day that was devised and appointed, the barons of renown assemble. King Arthur, together with the lords, whom he had chosen from out the good knights, lay before Oxford. Towards Wallingford went the greater part of his chivalry. Think not that I tell you in order to spin out my tale : such and such kings were there, such and such counts, and such and such others. When the barons were to meet, a knight of great prowess of King Arthur's peers rode out all alone between the two ranks to begin the tourney, as was the custom at that time. But none dares ride forward to come and joust against him. There is none who does not stay where he is, and yet there are some who ask : "Why do these knights wait, why does none ride forth from the ranks ? Surely someone will straightway begin." And on the other side they say : " See ye not what a champion our adversaries have sent us from their side ? Let him who has not yet known it know that of the four bravest known this is a pillar equal to the rest." " Who is he, then ? " " See ye him not ? It is Sagremors the Lawless." " Is it he ? " " Truly, without doubt." Cligés, who hears and hearkens to this, sat on Morel, and had armour blacker than a ripe mulberry : his whole armour was black. He separates himself from the others in the rank and

spurs Morel, who comes out of the row; not one is
there who sees him but says to his neighbour : "This
man rides well with feutred lance; here have we a
very skilful knight; he bears his arms in the right
fashion; well does the shield at his neck become him.
But one cannot but hold him mad as regards the joust
he has undertaken of his own accord against one of
the bravest known in all this land.  But who is he ?
Of what land is he a native ?  Who knows him ? "
"Not I!"  "Nor I!"  "But no snow has fallen
on him! rather is his armour blacker than monk's
or priest's cape."   Thus they engage in gossip,
and the two champions let their horses go, for no
longer do they delay, because right eager and aflame
are they for the encounter and the shock.  Cligés
strikes so that he presses Sagremors' shield to his arm
and his arm to his body.  Sagremors falls at full
length, Cligés acts irreproachably and makes him
declare himself prisoner : Sagremors gives his parole.
Now the fight begins, and they charge in rivalry.
Cligés has rushed to the combat and goes seeking
joust and encounter.  He encounters no knight whom
he does not take or lay low.  On both sides he wins
the highest distinction, for where he rides to joust he
brings the whole tourney to a standstill.  Yet he who
gallops up to joust with him is not without great

prowess ; but he wins more renown for standing his
ground against Cligés than for taking prisoner another
knight; and if Cligés leads him away captive, yet
he enjoys great distinction for merely daring to
withstand him in the joust. Cligés has the praise
and distinction of the whole tournament. At even
secretly he has returned to his lodging, so that none
of them might accost him about one thing or another.
And in case any one should have search made for
the lodging marked by the black arms, he locks them
up in a room, so that they may neither be found nor
seen, and he has the green arms openly displayed at
the door fronting the road, so that the passers by shall
see them. And if any asks for him and seeks him, he
will not know where his lodging will be, since he will
see no sign of the black shield that he seeks. Thus
Cligés is in the town and hides himself by such a
device. And those who were his prisoners went
from end to end of the town asking for the black
knight ; but none could tell them where he was.
And even King Arthur sends up and down to seek him ;
but all say : " We did not see him after we left the
tourney, and know not what became of him." More
than twenty youths whom the king has sent seek him ;
but Cligés has so utterly blotted out his tracks that
they find no sign of him. King Arthur crosses him-

self, when it was recounted and told him that neither great nor small is found who can point out his dwelling, any more than if he were at Cæsarea, or at Toledo or in Candia. " Faith ! " quoth he, " I know not what to say in the matter, but I marvel greatly thereat. It was perhaps a ghost that has moved among us. Many a knight has he overthrown to-day and he bears away the parole of the noblest, men who will not this year see home or land or country, and each of whom will have broken his oath." Thus the king spake his pleasure, though he might very well have kept silence in the matter.

Much have all the barons spoken that night of the black knight, for they spoke of nought else. On the morrow they returned to arms, all without summons and without entreaty. Lancelot of the Lake has dashed forth to make the first joust, for no coward is he ; with upright lance he awaits the joust. Lo ! Cligés, greener than meadow grass, galloping on a dun long-maned steed. Where Cligés pricks on the tawny steed, there is none, whether decked with youth's luxuriant locks or bald, who does not behold him with wonder, and they say on both sides : " This man is in all respects much nobler and more skilful than he of yesterday with the black arms, just as the pine is fairer than the beech and the laurel than the elder.

But not yet have we learned who he of yesterday was,
but we will learn this very day who this one is. If
anyone know it, let him tell us." Each said : " I
know him not, never did I see him before to my think-
ing. But he is fairer than the knight of yesterday, and
fairer than Lancelot of the Lake. If he were arrayed
in a sack and Lancelot in silver and gold, yet this man
would still be fairer." Thus all side with Cligés, and
the two prick their steeds as fast as they can spur,
and encounter one another. Cligés proceeds to deal
such a blow on the golden shield with the painted
lion, that he hurls its bearer from the saddle and fell
on him in order to receive his submission. Lancelot
could not defend himself, and has given his parole.
Then the noise and the din and the crash of lances
has begun. Those who were on Cligés' side have all
their trust in him ; for he whom he strikes, after due
challenge given, will never be so strong but that he
must needs fall from his horse to the ground. Cligés
this day wrought so bravely, and threw down and
captured so many, that he has pleased those on his side
twice as much and has had twice as much praise from
them as he had the day before. When evening has come,
he has repaired to his lodging as quickly as he could,
and speedily bids the red shield and the other armour
be brought forth. He orders that the arms which he

bore that day be stowed away; the landlord has carefully done it. Long have the knights whom he had captured sought him that night again, but no news do they hear of him. The greater part of those who speak of him at the inns laud and praise him.

Next day the knights return to arms alert and strong. From the array before Oxford rides out a knight of great renown, Percival the Welshman was he called. As soon as Cligés saw him ride forth, and heard the truth as to his name—for he heard him called Percival —he greatly longs to encounter him. Forthwith has he ridden forth from the rank on a sorrel Spanish steed, and his armour was red. Then they one and all regard him with great wonder more than they ever did before, and say that never before did they see so comely a knight. And the two prick forward at once, for there was no delay. And the one and the other spurs on, so that they give and take mighty blows on their shields. The lances, which were short and thick, bend and curve. In the sight of all who were looking on, Cligés has struck Percival so that he smites him down from his horse and makes him give parole without much fighting and without great ado. When Percival had submitted, then they have begun the tourney, and they all encounter together. Cligés encounters no knight but he fells him to the ground.

On this day one could not see him a single hour
absent from the fight.   Each for himself strikes a blow
at Cligés as though at a tower: not merely two or
three strike, for then that was not the use or custom.
Cligés has made an anvil of his shield, for all play the
smith, and hammer upon it, and cleave and quarter
it; but none strikes upon it but Cligés pays him back
and throws him from his stirrups and saddle, and no
one, except a man who wished to lie, could have said
on his departure that the knight with the red shield
had not won that whole day.   And the best and most
courteous would fain have his acquaintances; but
that cannot be so soon, for he has gone away secretly
when he saw that the sun had set, and he has had his
red shield and all his other armour taken away, and
he has the white arms brought, in which he had been
newly knighted; and the arms and the steed were
placed in front of the door.   But now they begin to
perceive (for the greater part who speak of it say so
and perceive it to be so) that they have all been dis-
comfited and put to flight by a single man, who
each day changes his outward show, both horse and
armour, and seems another than himself; they have
now for the first time perceived it.   And my lord
Gawain has said that never before did he see such a
jouster, and because he would fain have his acquaint-

ance and know his name, he says that he will be first
to-morrow at the encounter of the knights. But he
makes no boast; rather he says that he thinks and
believes that Cligés will have the best of it and will
win the renown when they strike with lances; but
with the sword perhaps Cligés will not be his master;
for never could Gawain find his master. Now will he
prove himself to-morrow on the strange knight, who
every day dons different armour and changes horse
and harness. Soon he will be a bird of many moult-
ings, if thus daily he makes a practice of taking off his
old feathers and putting on new ones. And thus
Gawain too doffed his armour, and put on other,
and the morrow he sees Cligés return whiter than lily-
flower, his shield held by the straps behind it, on his
trusty white Arab steed, as he had devised the night
before. Gawain, the valiant, the renowned, has not
gone to sleep on the field, but pricks and spurs and
advances and puts forth all his utmost efforts to joust
well, if he finds any with whom to joust. Soon both
will be on the field, for Cligés had no wish to delay,
for he had heard the murmur of those who say: " It
is Gawain, who is no weakling afoot or on horseback.
It is he with whom none dares to measure himself."
Cligés, who hears the words, charges into the middle
of the field towards him; both advance, and encounter

with a spring more swift than that of stag who hears
the baying of dogs barking after him. The lances
strike on the shields, and so mighty is the crash of the
blows that to their very ends they shatter into splinters,
and split and go to pieces, and the saddle-bows behind
break; moreover, the saddle-girth and breast-harness
burst. They both alike fall to the ground and have
drawn their naked swords. The folk have pressed
round to behold the battle. King Arthur came in
front of all to separate and reconcile them; but
they had broken and hewn in pieces the white
hauberks, and had cleft through and cut up the
shields and had fractured the helmets before there
was any talk of peace.

The king had gazed at them as long a time as it
pleased him, and so did many of the others, who
said that they esteemed the white knight no whit less
in arms than my lord Gawain, and up till now they
could not say which was the better, which the worse,
nor which would overcome the other, if they were
allowed to fight till the battle was fought out.
But it does not please or suit the king that they
do more than they have done. He advances to part
them, and says to them: "Withdraw! If another
blow be struck, it will be to your harm. But make
peace, be friends; fair nephew Gawain, I entreat you,

for it does not become a valiant man to continue a
battle or fight where he has no quarrel or hatred.
But if this knight would come to my court to pass
his time with us, it would be no grievance or hurt to
him. Pray him to do so, nephew." "Willingly,
Sire." Cligés seeks not to excuse himself from this;
willingly he consents to go thither, when the tourney
shall end, for now he has carried out to the uttermost
his father's command. And the king says that he
cares not for a tournament which lasts long; well
may they straightway leave it. The knights have
dispersed, for the king wishes and commands it.
Cligés sends for all his armour, for it behoves him to
follow the king. With all the speed he may he comes
to the court, but he was attired well beforehand and
garbed after the French fashion.

As soon as he came to court, each hastens to meet
him, for neither one nor the other remains behind,
rather they manifest the greatest possible joy and
festivity. And all those whom he had taken in the
jousting acclaim him lord, but it is his wish to dis-
claim it to all of them, and he says that, if they think
and believe that it was he who took them, they are
all absolved of their pledge. There is not a single
one who did not say: " It was you, well we know it.
We prize highly your acquaintance, and much ought

we to love you and esteem you and acclaim you lord,
for none of us is a match for you. Just as the sun
puts out the little stars, so that their light is not visible
in the clouds, where the rays of the sun shine forth,
so our deeds pale and wane before yours, and yet our
deeds were wont to be greatly renowned throughout
the world." Cligés knows not what reply to make
to them, for it seems to him that one and all of them
praise him more than they ought. Though it is
very pleasant to him, yet he is ashamed of it. The
blood rises into his face, so that they see him all
ashamed. They escort him through the hall and
have led him before the king; but they all cease to
address to him the language of praise and flattery.
Now was it the set hour for eating, and those whose
business it was hastened to set the tables. They
have set the tables in the palace: some have taken
napkins, and others hold basins and give water to
those who come. All have washed, all are seated.
The king has taken Cligés by the hand and set him
before him, for fain will he know this very day who he
is, if at all he may. No need is there to speak of the
food, for the dishes were as plentiful as though one
could have purchased an ox for a farthing.

When all had had their meat and drink, then has
the king no longer kept silence. " Friend," quoth

he, " I would know if it is from pride that you forbore
and disdained to come to my court as soon as you
entered this land, and why you thus withdraw your-
self from folk and change your arms.  Now impart
to me your name, and say of what race you are born."
Cligés replies : " Never shall it be concealed."  He
has told and related the king whatsoever he demands
from him ; and when the king has learned his name,
then he embraces him, then he rejoices over him ;
there is none who does not greet him in due form.
And my lord Gawain knew him, who above all
embraces and greets him.  All greet him and fall
on his neck, and all those who speak of him say that
he is right fair and valiant.  The king loves him and
honours him more than any of all his nephews.

Cligés stays with the king until the beginning of
summer ; by that time he has been over all Britain
and over France and over Normandy, and has wrought
many a knightly deed, so that he has well proved him-
self.  But the love with which he is wounded grows
neither lighter nor easier.  The wish of his heart
keeps him ever constant to one thought : he re-
members Fenice, who far from him is torturing her
heart.  A longing seizes him to return home, for too
long has he abstained from seeing the lady more
yearned for than any lady that ever heart of man has

yearned for. And he will not abstain longer from
her. He prepares for the journey to Greece, he has
taken leave and returns. Much I ween did it grieve
my lord Gawain and the king when they can no
longer keep him. But he longs to reach her whom he
loves and desires, and he hastens o'er sea and land,
and the way seems very long to him, so eagerly does
he yearn to see her who takes away and purloins his
heart from him. But she yields him a fair return,
and well does she pay and compensate him for the
toll she has extorted from him, for she, in her turn,
gives her own heart in payment to him, whom she
loves no less. But he is not a whit certain about it;
never had he pledge or promise in the matter, and he
grieves cruelly. And she also laments, for her love
of him is tormenting and killing her, and nothing
can give pleasure or joy in her eyes since that hour
when she ceased to see him. She does not even know
if he is alive, whereof great sorrow strikes her to
the heart. But Cligés gets nearer each day, and in
his journey he has had good luck, for he has had a
fair wind and calm weather, and has anchored with
joy and delight before Constantinople. The news
reached the city; it was welcome to the emperor and
a hundred times more welcome to the empress. If
anyone doubt this, it will be to his own sorrow.

Cligés and his company have repaired to Greece, straight to the port of Constantinople. All the most powerful and noble come to the port to meet him. And when the emperor, who had advanced in front of all, meets him, and the empress, who walks by his side, the emperor before all runs to fall on his neck and to greet him. And when Fenice greets him, the one changes colour because of the other, and the marvel is how, when they come close to each other, they keep from embracing and kissing each other with such kisses as please love. But folly would it have been and madness. The folk run up in all directions, and delight to see him. They all lead him through the midst of the town, some on foot and some on horseback, as far as the imperial palace. Of the joy that there was made will never word here be told, nor of the honour nor of the homage; but each has striven to do whatever he thinks and believes will please Cligés and be welcome to him. And his uncle yields to him all that he has, save the crown. He is right willing that Cligés take at his pleasure whatsoever he shall wish to obtain from him, be it land or treasure; but Cligés makes no account of silver or of gold, since he dare not disclose his thought to her for whom he loses his rest, and yet he has leisure and opportunity for telling her, if only he were not

afraid of being refused, for every day he can see her
and sit alone by her side without anyone gainsaying
or forbidding; for nobody imagines or thinks evil
of it.

A space of time after he had returned, one day he
came unattended into the room of her who was not
forsooth his enemy, and be well assured that the door
was not shut against the meeting.  He was close by
her side and all the rest had gone away, so that no
one was sitting near them who could hear their words.
Fenice first of all questioned him about Britain.
She asks him concerning the disposition and courtesy
of my lord Gawain, and at last she ventures to speak
of what she dreaded.  She asked him if he loved dame
or maiden in that land.  To this Cligés was not
unwilling or slow to reply.  Quickly was he able to
explain all to her, as soon as she challenged him on
the point.  "Lady," quoth he, "I was in love while
yonder, but I loved none who was of yonder land.
In Britain my body was without a heart like bark
without timber.  When I left Germany, I knew not
what became of my heart, save that it went away
hither after you.  Here was my heart and there my
body.  I was not absent from Greece, for my heart had
gone thither, and to reclaim it have I come back here;
but it neither comes nor returns to me, and I cannot

bring it back to me, and yet I seek it not and cannot do so. And how have you fared since you have come into this land ? What joy have you had here ? Do the people, does the land please you ? I ought to ask you nothing further save this—whether the land please you." " Formerly it pleased me not, but now there dawns for me a joy and a pleasure that I would not lose, be assured, for Pavia or for Placentia ; for I cannot dissever my heart from it, nor shall I ever use force to do so. In me is there nought save the bark, for without my heart I live and have my being. Never was I in Britain, and yet my heart has made I know not what contract in Britain without me." " Lady, when was your heart there ? Tell me when it went, at what time and at what season, if it is a matter that you can reasonably tell me or another. Was it there when I was there ? " " Yes, but you knew it not. It was there as long as you were there and departed with you." " God ! and I neither knew nor saw it there. God ! why did I know it not ? If I had known it, certainly, lady, I would have borne it good company." " Much would you have comforted me and well would it have become you to do so, for I would have been very gracious to your heart, if it had pleased it to come there where it might have known me to be." " Of a surety, lady,

it came to you." "To me? Then it came not into
exile, for mine also went to you." "Lady, then are
both our hearts here with us as you say; for mine
is wholly yours." "Friend, and you on your side
have mine, and so we are well matched. And know
well that, so may God guard me, never had your
uncle share in me, for neither did it please me nor
was it permitted to him. Never yet did he know
me as Adam knew his wife. Wrongly am I called
dame; but I know well that he who calls me dame
knows not that I am a maid. Even your uncle knows
it not, for he has drunk of the sleeping draught and
thinks he is awake when he sleeps, and he deems that
he has his joy of me, just as he fain would have it,
and just as though I were lying between his arms;
but well have I shut him out. Yours is my heart,
yours is my body, nor indeed will any one by my
example learn to act vilely; for when my heart set
itself on you, it gave and promised you my body,
so that nobody else shall have a share in it. Love
for you so wounded me that never did I think to
recover any more than the sea can dry up. If I love
you and you love me, never shall you be called
Tristram, and never shall I be Iseult, for then the
love would not be honourable. But I make you
a vow that never shall you have other solace of me

than you now have, if you cannot bethink yourself
how I may be stolen from your uncle and from his bed,
so that he may never find me again, or be able to
blame either you or me or have anything he may
lay hold of herein.  To-night must you bend your
attention to the matter and to-morrow you will be
able to tell me the best device that you will have
thought of, and I also will ponder on the matter.
To-morrow, when I shall have risen, come early to
speak to me, and each will say his thought, and we
will carry out that which we shall consider best."

When Cligés heard her wish, he has granted her
all, and says that it shall be right well done.  He
leaves her blithe, and blithe he goes away, and each
lies awake in bed all night and they think with
great delight over what seems best to them.  The
morrow they come again together, as soon as they
were risen, and they took counsel in private, as there
was need for them to do.  First Cligés says and re-
counts what he had thought of in the night.  "Lady,"
quoth he, "I think and believe that we could not
do better than go away to Britain : thither have I
devised to take you away.  Now take heed that the
matter fall not through on your side.  For never was
Helen received at Troy with such great joy, when
Paris had brought her thither, that there will not be

yet greater joy felt throughout the whole land of the
king, my uncle, anent you and me. And if this
please you not well, tell me your thought; for I am
ready, whatever come of it, to cleave to your thought."
She replies: " And I shall speak it. Never will I
go with you thus, for then, when we had gone away,
we should be spoken of throughout the world as
the blonde Iseult and Tristram are spoken of; but
here and there all women and men would blame our
happiness. No one would believe or could be ex-
pected to believe the actual truth of the matter.
Who would believe then as regards your uncle that I
have gone off and escaped from him still a maid, but
a maid to no purpose ? Folk would hold me a light-
of-love and a wanton, and you a madman. But it
is meet to keep and observe the command of St. Paul,
for St. Paul teaches him who does not wish to remain
continent to act so wisely that he may never incur
outcry nor blame nor reproach. It is well to stop
an evil mouth, and this I think I can fully accomplish,
if it be not too grievous for you; for if I act as my
thought suggests to me, I will pretend to be dead.
I will shortly feign sickness, and do you on your side
lavish your pains to provide for my tomb. Set
your attention and care on this, that both tomb
and bier be made in such fashion that I die not

there nor suffocate, and let no one perceive you
that night when you will be ready to take me away.
And you will find me a refuge, such that never any
save you may see me; and let no one provide me
with anything of which I have need or require-
ment, save you to whom I grant and give myself.
Never in all my life do I seek to be served by any
other man. You will be my lord and my servant,
good will be to me whatsoever you will do to me,
nor shall I ever be lady of the empire, if you be not
lord of it. A poor, dark, and sordid place will be to
me more splendid than all these halls, when you shall
be together with me. If I have you and see you, I
shall be lady of all the wealth in the world, and the
whole world will be mine. And if the thing is done
wisely, never will it be interpreted ill, and none will
ever be able to point the finger of scorn at me, for
through the whole empire folk will believe that I have
rotted in the grave. And Thessala, my nurse, who
has brought me up and in whom I have great trust, will
aid me in good faith, for she is very wise and I have
great confidence in her." And Cligés, when he
heard his love, replies: "Lady, if so it can be, and if
you think that your nurse is likely to counsel you
rightly in the matter, all you have to do is to make
preparations and to carry them out speedily; but if

we act not wisely, we are lost beyond recovery. In this town there is a craftsman who carves and works in wood wondrous well; there is no land where he is not famed for the works of art that he has made and carved and shaped. John is his name, and he is my serf. No handicraft is there, however peculiar it be, in which anyone could rival him, if John set his mind to it with a will. For compared with him they are all novices like a child at nurse. It is by imitating his works that the inhabitants of Antioch and of Rome have learned to do whatever they can accomplish, and no more loyal man is known. But now will I put him to the test, and if I can find loyalty in him, I will free him and all his heirs, and I will not fail to tell him our plan, if he swears and vows to me that he will aid me loyally therein and will never betray me in this matter." She replies : " Now be it so."

By her leave Cligés came forth from the chamber and departed. And she sends for Thessala, her nurse, whom she had brought from the land where she was born. And Thessala came forthwith, for she neither lingers nor delays : but she knows not why her mistress sends for her. Fenice asks her in private conference what she counsels and what seems good to her. She neither hides nor conceals from Thessala even the smallest part of her thought.

" Nurse," says she, " I know well that never a thing
that I tell you will afterwards become known through
you, for I have proved you right well and have found
you very wise. You have done so much for me that I
love you. Of all my evils I complain to you, nor do I
take counsel elsewhere. You know well why I lie awake
and what I think and what I wish. My eyes can see
nothing to please me, save one thing, but I shall have
from it neither enjoyment nor comfort, if I do not
pay very dearly for it beforehand. And yet I have
found my mate ; for if I desire him, he, on his side,
desires me too ; if I grieve, he, on his side, grieves
with my sorrow and my anguish. Now I must
confess to you a thought and a parley, in which we
two in solitude have resolved and agreed." Then
she has told and related to her that she intends to
feign herself ill, and says that she will complain so
much that finally she will appear dead, and Cligés
will steal her away in the night, and they will be
always henceforth together. In no other way, it
seems to her, could she continue firm in her resolve.
But if she were assured that Thessala would help
her in it, the thing could be done according to
her wish ; " but too long do joy and good fortune
for me delay and tarry." Forthwith her nurse assures
her that she will lend all her aid to the enterprise,

let her now have neither fear nor dread in regard to aught; and she says she will take so much pains about the matter, as soon as she shall undertake it, that never will there be any man who sees her who will not believe quite surely that her soul is severed from the body, when Thessala shall have given her a drink that will make her cold and wan and pale and stiff, without speech and without breath; and yet she will be quite alive and sound, and will feel neither good nor ill, nor will she suffer any harm during a day and a whole night in the tomb and in the bier.

When Fenice had heard it, thus has she spoken and replied: "Nurse, I put myself in your care, I give you free leave to do what you will with me. I am at your disposal; think for me, and bid the folk here that there be none who does not go away. I am ill and they disturb me." The nurse tells them courteously: "My lords, my lady is unwell and wishes you all to go away, for you speak too much and make too much noise, and noise is bad for her. She will have neither rest nor ease as long as you are in this room. Never heretofore that I remember had she illness of which I heard her complain so much, so very great and grievous is her sickness. Depart, an it vex you not." They speedily go, one and all, as soon as Thessala had commanded it. And Cligés

has quickly sent for John to his lodging, and has said
to him privily : "John, knowest thou what I will
say ? Thou art my serf, I am thy lord, and I can
give thee or sell thee and take thy body and thy goods
as a thing that is my own. But if I could trust thee
concerning an affair of mine that I am thinking of,
thou wouldst for evermore be free, and likewise the
heirs which shall be born of thee." John, who much
desires freedom, forthwith replies : " Sir," says he,
" there is no thing that I would not do wholly at
your will, provided that thereby I might see myself
free and my wife and children free. Tell me your
will ; never will there be anything so grievous that it
will be toil or punishment to me, nor will it be any
burden to me. And were it not so, yet it will behove
me to do it even against my will, and set aside all
my own business." " True, John, but it is such a
thing that my mouth dare not speak it, unless thou
warrant me and swear to me, and unless thou alto-
gether assure me that thou wilt faithfully aid me and
will never betray me." " Willingly, Sir," quoth
John, " never be doubtful of that. For this I swear
you and warrant you that as long as I shall be a living
man I will never say aught that I think will grieve
or vex you." " Ah, John ! not even on pain of death
is there a man to whom I should dare to say that

concerning which I wish to seek counsel of thee;
rather would I let my eyes be plucked out. Rather
would I that thou shouldst kill me than that thou
shouldst say it to any other man. But I find thee so
leal and prudent, that I will tell thee what is in my
heart. Thou wilt accomplish my pleasure well, as
I think, as regards both thy aid and thy silence."
"Truly, Sir! so aid me God!" Forthwith Cligés
relates to him and tells him the enterprise quite openly.
And when he has disclosed to him the truth, as ye
know it who have heard me tell it, then John says
that he promises him to make the tomb well and put
therein his best endeavour, and says that he will take
him to see a house of his own building, and he will
show him this that he has made, which never any
man, woman, or child yet saw, if it pleases him to go
with him there where he is working and painting and
carving all by himself without any other folk. He
will show him the fairest and most beautiful place that
he ever saw. Cligés replies: "Let us then go."

Below the town in a sequestered spot had John
built a tower, and he had toiled with great wisdom.
Thither has he led Cligés with him, and leads him over
the rooms, which were adorned with images fair and
finely painted. He shows him the rooms and the
fireplaces, and leads him up and down. Cligés sees

the house to be lonely, for no one stays or dwells there.
He passes from one room to another till he thinks to
have seen all, and the tower has pleased him well, and
he said that it was very beautiful.  The lady will be
safe there all the days that she will live ; for no man
will ever know her to be there.  " No, truly, lord, she
will never be known to be here.  But think you to have
seen all my tower and all my pleasaunce ?  Still are
there lurking-places such as no man would be able
to find.  And if it is allowed you to try your skill in
searching as well as you can, never will you be able to
ransack so thoroughly as to find more rooms here, how-
ever subtle and wise you are, if I do not show and point
them out to you.  Know that here baths are not
lacking, nor anything that I remember and think of
as suitable for a lady.  She will be well at her ease
here.  This tower has a wider base underground,
as you shall see, and never will you be able to find
anywhere door or entrance.  With such craft and such
art is the door made of hard stone that never will
you find the join thereof."  " Now hear I marvels,"
quoth Cligés ; " go forward ; I shall follow, for I long
to see all this."  Then has John started off, and leads
Cligés by the hand to a smooth and polished door,
which is all painted and coloured.  At the wall has
John stopped, and he held Cligés by the right hand.

" Lord," quoth he, " no man is there who could have
seen door or window in this wall, and think you that
one could pass it in any wise without doing it injury
and harm ? "   Cligés answers that he does not think
he could, nor ever will think it, unless he sees it
with his own eyes.   Then says John that his lord
shall see it, for he will open for him the door of the
wall.   John, who himself had wrought the work, un-
locks and opens to him the door of the wall, so that he
neither hurts it nor injures it, and the one passes
before the other, and they descend by a spiral stair-
case to a vaulted room where John wrought at his
craft, when it was his pleasure to construct aught.
" Lord," quoth he, " here where we are was never one
of all the men whom God created save us two ;  and
the place has all that makes for comfort, as you will
see in a trice.   I advise that your retreat be here, and
that your lady-love be hidden in it.   Such a lodging is
meet for such a guest, for there are rooms and baths
and in the baths hot water, which comes through a
pipe below the earth.   That man who would seek a
convenient spot to place and hide his lady would
have to go far before he found one so delightful.
You will deem it a very fitting refuge when you
have been all over it."   Then has John shown him
all, fair chambers and painted vaults, and he has shown

him much of his workmanship, which pleased him
mightily. When they had seen the whole tower,
then said Cligés : " John, my friend, I free you and
your heirs one and all, and I am wholly yours. I
desire that my lady be here all alone, and that no one
ever know it save me and you and her, and not another
soul." John replies : " I thank you. Now we have
been here long enough, now we have no more to do,
so let us start on the return journey." " You have
said well," Cligés replies, " let us depart." Then
they turn and have issued forth from the tower.
On their return they hear in the town how one tells
another in confidence : " You know not the grave news
about my lady the empress. May the Holy Spirit
give health to the wise and noble lady, for she lies in
very great sickness."

When Cligés hears the report, he went to the court
at full speed ; but neither joy nor pleasure was there
there ; for all were sad and dejected on account of
the empress, who feigns herself ill ; feigns—for the
evil whereof she complains gives her no pain or
hurt ; she has said to all that as long as the malady
whereby her heart and head feel pain holds her so
strongly, she will have no man save the emperor or
his nephew enter her chamber ; for she will not
deny herself to them ; though if the emperor, her

lord, come not, little will it irk her. She must needs risk great suffering and great peril for Cligés' sake, but it weighs on her heart that he comes not; she desires to see naught save him. Cligés will soon be in her presence and stay there till he shall have related to her what he has seen and found. He comes before her and has told her; but he remained there a short time only, for Fenice, in order that people may think that what pleases her annoys her, has said aloud: "Away! Away! You tire me greatly, you weary me much; for I am so oppressed with sickness that never shall I be raised from it and restored to health." Cligés, whom this greatly pleases, goes away, making a doleful countenance—for never before did you see it so doleful. Outwardly he appears full sad; but his heart is blithe within, for it looks to have its joy.

The empress, without having any illness, complains and feigns herself ill; and the emperor, who believes her, ceases not to make lamentation, and sends to seek leeches for her; but she will not that one see her, nor does she let herself be touched. This grieves the emperor, for she says that never will she have leech except one, who will know how to give her health quickly, when it shall be his will. He will make her die or live; into his keeping she puts herself for health and for life. They think that she is speaking of God, but a very different meaning has she, for she means none other than Cligés. He is her God, who can give her health and who can make her die.

Thus the empress provides that no leech attend her, and she will not eat or drink, in order the better to deceive the emperor, until she is both pale and wan all over. And her nurse stays near her, who with very wondrous craft sought secretly through all the town, so that no one knew it, until she found a woman sick of a mortal sickness without cure. In order the better to carry out the deception, she went often to visit her and promised her that she would cure her of her ill, and each day she would bring a glass to see her water, till she saw that medicine would no longer be able to aid her and that she would die that very day. She has brought this water and has kept it straitly until the emperor rose. Now she goes before him and says to him : " If you will, sire, send for all your leeches, for my lady, who is suffering from a sore sickness, has passed water and wishes that the leeches see it, but that they come not in her presence." The leeches came into the hall; they see the water very bad and pale, and each says what seems to him the truth, till they all agree together that never will she recover, and will not even see the hour of None, and

if she lives so long, then at the latest God will take her
soul to himself. This have they murmured secretly.
Then the emperor has bidden and conjured them
that they tell the truth of the matter. They reply
that they have no hope at all of her recovery, and
that she cannot pass the hour of None, for before
that hour she will have given up the ghost. When
the emperor has heard the word, scarcely can he refrain
from swooning to the ground, and likewise many a one
of the others who heard it. Never did any folk make
such mourning as then prevailed through all the
palace. I spare you the account of the mourning,
and you shall hear what Thessala is about, who mixes
and brews the draught. She has mixed and stirred
it, for long beforehand she had provided herself with
all that she knew was needed for the draught. A
little before the hour of None she gives her the draught
to drink. As soon as she had drunk it, her sight grew
dim, and her face was as pale and white as if she had
lost her blood, nor would she have moved hand or foot
even if one had flayed her alive; she neither stirs nor
says a word, and yet she hearkens to and hears the
mourning which the emperor makes, and the wailing
with which the hall is full. And o'er all the city the
folk wail who weep and say : " God ! what a sorrow
and a calamity has accursed death dealt us ! Greedy

death! covetous death! Death is worse than any
she-wolf, for death cannot be sated. Never couldst
thou give a worse wound to the world. Death, what
hast thou done? May God confound thee who hast
extinguished all beauty. Thou hast slain the choicest
creature and the fairest picture—if she had but re-
mained alive!—that God ever laboured to fashion.
Too patient is God, since He suffers thee to have the
power to ruin His handiwork. Now should God be
wroth with thee and cast thee forth from thy domin-
ion, for thou hast committed too wanton and great
arrogance and great insult." Thus all the people
storm, they wring their hands and beat their palms,
and the clerks read there their psalms, who pray for
the good lady that God may show mercy to her soul.

Amid the tears and the wails, as the writings tell us,
have come three aged physicians from Salerno, where
they had been long time. They have stopped on
account of the great mourning, and ask and inquire the
reason of the wails and tears, why folk are thus demented
and distressed. And they tell them and reply: "God!
lords, know ye not? At this ought the whole world,
each place in turn, to become frenzied together with
us, if it knew the great mourning and grief and hurt
and the great loss which this day has opened to our
ken. God! whence then are you come, since you

know not what has happened but now in the city ?
We will tell you the truth, for we wish to join you
with us in the mourning wherewith we mourn.
Know you nought of ravenous death, who desires all
and covets all and in all places lies in wait for the
best, and how great an act of folly he hath to-day
committed, as he is wont ?  God had lit the world
with a brilliance, with a light.  But Death cannot
choose but do what he is wont to do.  Ever with his
might he blots out the best that he can find.  Now
doth he will to prove his power, and has taken in
one body more worth than he has left in the world.
If he had taken the whole world, he could not have
done one whit worse, provided that he left alive and
sound that prey whom he now leads away.  Beauty,
courtesy, and knowledge, and whatsoever appertaining
to goodness a lady can have, has Death, who has de-
stroyed all good in the person of my lady the empress,
snatched from us and cheated us of.  Thus hath
Death slain us."  " Ah, God ! " say the leeches, " thou
hatest this city, we know it well, for that we came
not here a little space ago.  If we had come yester-
day, Death might have esteemed himself highly, if
he had taken aught from us by force."  " Lords, my
lady would not for aught have allowed that you
should have seen her or troubled yourself about

her.  There were enough and to spare of good leeches, but never did my lady please that one or other of them should see her who could meddle with her illness."  " No ? "  " By my faith, that did she truly not."  Then they remembered Solomon, and that his wife hated him so much that she betrayed him under a pretence of death.  Perhaps this lady has done the same thing; but if they could by any means succeed in touching her, there is no man born for whose sake they would have lied or would refrain from speaking the whole truth about it, if they can see deceit there. Towards the court they go forthwith, where one would not have heard God thundering, such noise and wailing there was.  The master of them, who knew the most, has approached the bier.  None says to him : " You touch it at your peril."  Nor does any one pull him back from it.  And he puts his hand on her breast and on her side and feels beyond a doubt that she has her life whole in her body; well he knows it and well he perceives it.  He sees before him the emperor, who is frenzied and ready to kill himself with grief.  He cries aloud and says to him : " Emperor, comfort thyself.  I know and see for a certainty that this lady is not dead. Leave thy mourning and console thyself.  If I give her not back to thee alive, either slay me or hang me."

Now all the wailing throughout the palace is calmed

and hushed, and the emperor tells the leech that now
it is permitted him to give orders and to speak his will
quite freely.    If he brings back the empress to life, he
will be lord and commander over him ; but he will be
hanged as a robber, if he has lied to him in aught.
And he says to him : " I accept the condition ; never
have mercy on me, if I do not make the lady here speak
to you.    Without hesitation or delay have the palace
cleared for me.    Let not one or another stay here.    I
must see privately the evil from which the lady suffers.
These two leeches alone, who are of my company,
shall stay here with me, and let all the others go with-
out."    This thing Cligés, John, and Thessala would
have gainsaid : but all those who were there would
have interpreted it to their harm, if they had attempted
to prevent it.    Therefore they keep silence and give
the counsel that they hear the others give, and have
gone forth from the palace.    And the three leeches
have by force ripped up the lady's winding-sheet, for
there was neither knife nor scissors : then they say :
" Lady, have no fear, be not dismayed, but speak in all
safety.    We know for a surety that you are quite sound
and well.    Now be wise and amenable, and despair of
nought ; for if you seek advice from us, we will assure
you all three of us, that we will help you with all
our power, where it be concerning good or concern-

ing evil.   We will be right loyal towards you, both in keeping your secret and in aiding you.   Do not compel us to reason long with you.   From the moment that we place our power and services at your disposal, you ought not to refuse us compliance."   Thus they think to befool and to cheat her, but it avails nought ; for she cares and recks nought of the service that they promise her ; they are meddling to no purpose.   And when the physicians see that they will avail nothing with regard to her by cajolery or by entreaty, then they take her off the bier and strike her and beat her ; but their fury is to no purpose, since for all this they draw not a word from her.   Then they threaten and frighten her and say that, if she does not speak, she will that very day find out the folly of her action ; for they will inflict on her such dire treatment that never before was its like inflicted on any body of caitiff woman.   "Well we know that you are alive and do not deign to speak to us.   Well we know that you are feigning and would have deceived the emperor.   Have no fear of us at all. But if any man has angered you, disclose your folly, before we have further wounded you, for you are acting very basely ; and we will aid you, alike in wisdom or in folly."   It cannot be, it avails them nought.   Then once more they deal her blows on the back with their straps, and the stripes that run down-

wards become visible, and so much do they beat her
tender flesh that they make the blood gush out from it.

When they have beaten her with straps till they have
lacerated her flesh, and till the blood which issues
through her wounds runs down from them, and when
for all that they can do nothing nor extort sigh or word
from her, and she never moves nor stirs, then they
tell her that they must seek fire and lead, and that they
will melt it and will pour it into her palms rather than
fail to make her speak.  They seek and search for fire
and lead; they kindle the fire; they melt the lead.
Thus the base villains maltreat and torture the lady,
for they have poured into her palms the lead, all boil-
ing and hot just as they have taken it from the fire.
Nor yet is it enough for them that the lead has passed
through and through the palms, but the reprobate
villains say that, if she speak not soon, straightway
they will roast her till she is all grilled.  She is silent
and forbids them not to beat or ill-treat her flesh.  And
even now they were about to put her to the fire to
roast and grill, when more than a thousand of the
ladies, who were in front of the palace, come to the
door and see through a tiny chink the torture and the
unhappy fate that they were preparing for the lady,
for they were making her suffer martyrdom from the
coal and from the flame.  To break in the door and

shatter it they bring hatchets and hammers. Great
was the din and the attack to break and smash the
door. If now they can lay hold on the leeches,
without delay all their desert shall be rendered them.
The ladies enter the palace all together with one bound,
and Thessala is among the press, whose one anxiety
is to get to her lady. She finds her all naked at the
fire, much injured and much mishandled. She has
laid her back on the bier and covered her beneath the
pall. And the ladies proceed to tender and pay to
the three leeches their deserts; they would not send
for or await emperor or seneschal. They have hurled
them down through the windows full into the court,
so that they have broken the necks and ribs and arms
and legs of all three; better never wrought any ladies.

Now the three leeches have received from the
ladies right sorry payment for their deeds; but Cligés
is much dismayed and has great grief, when he hears
tell of the great agony and the torture that his lady
has suffered for him. Almost does he lose his reason;
for he fears greatly—and indeed with justice—that
she may be killed or maimed by the torture caused
her by the three leeches, who have died in conse-
quence; and he is despairing and disconsolate. And
Thessala comes bringing a very precious salve with
which she has anointed full gently the lady's body and

wounds. The ladies have enshrouded her again in a white Syrian pall, wherein they had shrouded her before, but they leave her face uncovered. Never that night do they abate their wailing or cease or make an end thereof. Through all the town they wail like folk demented—high and low, and poor and rich—and it seems that each sets his will on outdoing all the others in making lamentation, and on never abandoning it of his own will. All night is the mourning very great. On the morrow John came to court, and the emperor sends for him and bids him, requests and commands him: "John! if ever thou madest a good work, now set all thy wisdom and thy invention to making a tomb, such that one cannot find one so fair and well decorated." And John, who had already done it, says that he has prepared a very fair and well-carved one; but never, when he began to make it, had he intention that any body should be laid there save a holy one. "Now, let the empress be enclosed within in lieu of relics; for she is, I ween, a very holy thing." "Well said," quoth the emperor: "in the minster of my lord Saint Peter shall she be buried, there outside where one buries other bodies; for before she died, she begged and prayed me with all her heart that I would have her laid there. Now go and busy yourself about it, and

set your tomb, as is right and meet, in the fairest
place in the cemetery." John replies: "Gladly,
sire." Forthwith John departs, prepares well the
tomb, and did thereat what a master of his craft would
do. Because the stone was hard, and even more on
account of the cold, he has placed therein a feather
bed; and moreover, that it may smell sweet to her,
he has strewn thereon both flowers and foliage. But
he did it even more for this, that none should spy
the mattress that he had placed in the grave. Now
had the whole office been said in chapels and in
parish churches, and they were continually tolling as
it is meet to toll for the dead. They bid the body
be brought, and it will be placed in the tomb, whereat
John has worked to such effect that he has made it
very magnifical and splendid. In all Constantinople
has been left neither great nor small who does not
follow the corpse weeping, and they curse and revile
Death; knights and squires swoon, and the dames and
the maidens beat their breasts and have railed against
Death. "Death!" quoth each, "why took'st thou
not a ransom for my lady? Forsooth, but a small
booty hast thou gained, and for us the loss is great."
And Cligés, of a truth, mourns so much that he wounds
and maltreats himself more than all the others do,
and it is a marvel that he does not kill himself; but

still he postpones suicide till the hour and the time
come for him to disinter her and hold her in his
arms, and know whether she is alive or not.   About
the grave are the lords, who lay the body there ; but
they do not meddle with John in the setting up of
the tomb, and indeed they could see nought of it,
but have all fallen swooning to the earth, and John
has had good leisure to do all he listed.   He so set
up the tomb that there was no other creature
in it ; well does he seal and join and close it.
Then might that man well have boasted himself who,
without harm or injury, would have been able to
take away or disjoin aught that John had put there.

Fenice is in the tomb, until it came to dark night ;
but thirty knights guard her, and there are ten tapers
burning, and they made a great light.   The knights
were sated and weary with mourning, and have eaten
and drunk in the night till they all lay asleep together.
At night Cligés steals forth from the court and from
all the folk.   There was not knight or servant who
ever knew what had become of him.   He did not
rest till he came to John, who gives him all the counsel
that he can.   He puts on him a suit of armour, which
he will never need.   Both all armed go forth to the
cemetery at post haste : but the cemetery was en-
closed all around by a high wall ; and the knights,

who were sleeping, and had closed the door within
that none might enter, thought they were safe.
Cligés sees not how he may pass, for he cannot enter
by the door, and yet by hook or by crook he must enter,
for love exhorts and admonishes him. He grips the
wall and mounts up, for right strong and agile was he.
Within was an orchard and there were trees in plenty.
Near the wall one had been planted so that it touched
the wall. Now has Cligés what he wished for; he
let himself down by this tree. The first thing that
he did was to go and open the door to John. They
see the knights sleeping, and they have extinguished
all the tapers, so that no light remains there. And
now John uncovers the grave and opens the tomb, so
that he injures it not at all. Cligés leaps into the
grave and has carried forth his lady, who is very
weak and lifeless, and he falls on her neck and
kisses and embraces her. He knows not whether
to rejoice or mourn; for she moves not nor stirs.
And John has closed again the tomb with all the
speed he may, so that it does not in any wise appear
that it had been touched. They have approached the
tower as quickly as ever they could. When they had
put her within the tower in the rooms that were under-
ground, then they took off the grave-clothes, and Cligés,
who knew nothing of the draught that she had within

her body, which makes her dumb and prevents her
stirring, thinks in consequence that she is dead, and he
loses hope and comfort thereat, and sighs deeply and
weeps.  But soon the hour will have come that the
draught will lose its force.  And Fenice, who hears
him lament, tries and strains that she may be able to
comfort him either by word or by look.  Her heart
nearly breaks because of the mourning she hears him
make.  "Ha! Death," quoth he, "how base thou art, in
that thou sparest and passest by worthless and outcast
creatures !  Such thou dost allow to last and live.
Death !  art thou mad or drunk that thou has killed my
love without killing me ?   This that I see is a marvel :
my love is dead and I am alive.  Ah, sweet love !  why
does your lover live and see you dead ?   Now might
one rightly say that you are dead for my sake, and that
I have killed and slain you.  Loved lady !  then am I
the Death who has killed you ;  is not that unjust ?
For I have taken away my life in you and yet have
kept yours in me.  For were not your health and your
life mine, sweet friend ?   And were not mine yours ?
For I loved nought but you : we twain were one
being.  Now have I done what I ought, for I keep
your soul in my body, and mine is gone forth of yours ;
and yet the one was bound to bear the other com-
pany, wherever it was, and nothing ought to have

parted them." At this she heaves a sigh and says in a weak, low voice: "Friend! friend! I am not wholly dead, but well-nigh so. But I hope nought about my life. I thought to have a jest and to feign: but now must I needs complain, for Death loves not my jest. A marvel 'twill be if I escape alive, for much have the leeches wounded me, broken and lacerated my flesh; and nevertheless, if it could be that my nurse were here with me, she would make me quite whole, if care could avail aught herein." "Friend! then let it not distress you," quoth Cligés, "for this very night I will bring her here for you." "Friend! rather will John go." John goes thither and has sought till he found her, and he imparts to her how greatly he desires her to come; never let any excuse detain her; for Fenice and Cligés summon her to a tower where they await her; for Fenice is sore mishandled, and she must come provided with salves and electuaries, and let her know that the lady will live no longer if she succour her not speedily. Thessala forthwith runs and takes ointment and plaster and electuary that she had made, and has joined company with John. Then they issue from the town secretly and go till they come straight to the tower. When Fenice sees her nurse, she thinks she is quite cured, so much she loves her and believes in her and trusts her. And Cligés embraces and greets

her and says : " Welcome, nurse ! for I love and
esteem you greatly. Nurse, in God's name what
think you of this damsel's illness ? What is your
opinion ? Will she recover ? " " Ay, sir ! fear not
that I cannot cure her right well. A fortnight will
not have passed before I make her whole, so that
never at any time was she more whole and gay."

Thessala sets her mind on curing the lady, and
John goes to provide the tower with whatsoever
store is meet. Cligés comes and goes to the tower
boldly, in view of all, for he has left there a goshawk
moulting, and says that he comes to see it, and none
can guess that he goes there for any other reason
save only on account of the hawk. Much does he
tarry there both night and day. He makes John
guard the tower, that no one may enter there against
his will. Fenice has no hurt whereof she need grieve,
for well has Thessala cured her. If now Cligés had
been duke of Almeria or of Morocco or of Tudela, he
would not have prized such honour a berry in com-
parison of the joy he has. Certes, love abased himself
no whit when he put them together ; for it seems to
both when one embraces and kisses the other that the
whole world is made better for their joy and their
pleasure. Ask me no more about it ; I will but say
that there is nought that one wills that the other does

not welcome.  So is their will at one as if they twain
were but one.

All this year and some space of the next, two months
and more, I ween, has Fenice been in the tower,
until the spring of the year.  When flowers and
foliage bud forth, and the little birds are making
merry—for they delight in their bird-language
—it happened that Fenice heard one morning the
nightingale sing.  Cligés was holding her gently with
one arm about her waist and the other about her neck,
and she him in like manner, and she has said to him :
" Fair, dear friend, much joy would an orchard afford
me, where I could take my pleasure.  I have seen
neither moon nor sun shine for more than fifteen
whole months.  If it might be, full gladly would I
sally forth into the daylight, for I am pent up in this
tower.  If near by there were an orchard where I
could go to disport myself, great good would this do
me often.  Then Cligés promises that he will seek
counsel of John as soon as he shall see him.  And now
it has happened that lo ! John has come thither,
for he was often wont to come.  Cligés has spoken
with him of Fenice's desire.  " All is prepared and
already at hand," quoth John, " whatsoever she
orders.  This tower is well provided with all that she
wishes and asks for."  Then is Fenice right blithe

and bids John lead her thither, and John makes no demur. Then goes John to open a door, such that I have neither skill nor power to tell or describe the fashion of it. None save John could have had the skill to make it, nor could any one ever have told that there was door or window there, as long as the door was not opened, so hidden and concealed was it.

When Fenice saw the door open and the sun which she had not seen for a long time shine in, she has all her blood awhirl with joy and says that now she seeks nothing more, inasmuch as she can come forth out of the hiding-place, and seeks no refuge elsewhere. By the door she has entered the orchard, and this greatly pleases and delights her. In the midst of the orchard there was a grafted tree loaded with flowers and very leafy, and it formed a canopy above. The branches were so trained that they hung towards the ground and bent almost to the earth, all save the top from which they sprang, for that rose straight upwards. Fenice desires no other place. And below the grafted tree the meadow is, very delectable and very fair, nor ever will the sun be so high even at noon, when it is hottest, that ever a ray can pass that way, so skilled was John to arrange things and to guide and train the branches. There Fenice goes to disport herself, and all day she makes her couch there ; there they are

in joy and delight.    And the orchard is enclosed
around with a high wall which joins the tower, so
that no creature could enter it, unless he had climbed
to the top of the tower.

Now is Fenice in great delight: there is nought
to displease her, nor lacks she aught that she could
wish, when 'neath the flowers and leaves it lists her
embrace her lover.    At the time when folk go hunting
with the sparrow-hawk and with the hound, which
seeks the lark and the stonechat and tracks the quail
and the partridge, it happened that a knight of
Thrace, a young and sprightly noble, esteemed for
his prowess, had one day gone a-hawking quite close
beside this tower; Bertrand was the knight's name.
His sparrow-hawk had soared high, for it had missed
the lark that was its aim.    Now will Bertrand con-
sider himself ill served by fate, if he lose his sparrow-
hawk.    He saw it descend and settle below the tower
in an orchard, and it pleased him much to see this,
for now he reckons that he will not lose it.    Forthwith
he goes to scale the wall, and wins to get over it.
Under the grafted tree he saw Fenice and Cligés
sleeping together side by side.    " God ! " quoth he,
" what has befallen me ?    What kind of miracle is it
that I see ?    Is it not Cligés ?    Yea, i'faith.    Is
not that the empress by his side ?    Nay, but she

resembles her, for no other being ever was so like.
Such a nose, such a mouth, such a brow she has as
the empress, my lady, had. Never did nature better
succeed in making two beings of the same countenance.
In this lady see I nought that I should not have seen
in my lady. If she had been alive, truly I should have
said that it was she." At that moment a pear drops
and falls just beside Fenice's ear. She starts, awakes,
sees Bertrand and cries aloud : " Friend, friend, we
are lost ! Here is Bertrand ! If he escapes you, we
have fallen into an evil trap. He will tell folk that he
has seen us." Then has Bertrand perceived that it
is the empress beyond all doubt. Need is there for
him to depart, for Cligés had brought his sword with
him into the orchard, and had laid it beside the couch.
He springs up and has taken his sword, and Bertrand
flees swiftly. With all the speed he might he grips
the wall, and now he was all but over it, when Cligés
has come after, raises now his sword, and strikes him,
so that beneath the knee he has cut off his leg as clean
as a stalk of fennel. Nevertheless, Bertrand has
escaped ill-handled and crippled, and on the other
side he is received by his men, who are beside them-
selves with grief and wrath, when they see him thus
maimed ; they have asked and inquired who it is
that had done it to him. " Question me not about

it," quoth he, " but raise me on my horse. Never
will this story be recounted till it is told before the
emperor. He who has done this to me ought not
forsooth to be without fear—nor is he, for he is nigh
to deadly peril." Then they have put him on his
palfrey, and, mourning, they lead him away in great
dismay through the midst of the town. After them
go more than twenty thousand, who follow him to
the court. And all the people flock there, the one
after the other, and the devil take the hindmost.

Now has Bertrand made his plea and complaint to
the emperor in the hearing of all, but they consider
him an idle babbler because he says that he has seen
the empress stark naked. All the town is stirred
thereat ; some, when they hear this news, esteem it
mere folly, others advise and counsel the emperor to
go to the tower. Great is the uproar and the tumult
of the folk who set out after him. But they find
nothing in the tower, for Fenice and Cligés are on
their way, and have taken Thessala with them, who
comforts and assures them, and says that, even if
perchance they see folk coming after them who come
to take them, they need have no fear for aught, for
never to do them harm or injury would they come
within the distance that one could shoot with a strong
crossbow stretched by windlass.

Now the emperor is in the tower and he has John
sought out and fetched : he bids that he be tied and
bound, and says that he will have him hanged or
burned and the ashes scattered to the wind.   For the
shame that the emperor has suffered, John shall pay
the penalty (but it will be a bootless penalty !), because
he has secreted in his tower the nephew and the wife of
the emperor.   " I'faith you speak the truth," quoth
John ; " I will not lie in the matter ; I will stick to the
truth throughout, and if I have done wrong in any
point, right meet is it that I be taken.   But on this
score I could well excuse myself, that a serf ought to
refuse nought that his rightful lord commands him.
And it is known full surely that I am his and the
tower is his."   " Nay, John, rather is it thine."
" Mine, sire ?   Truly, as his serf I am not even my
own, nor have I anything that is mine, save in so far
as he grants it to me.   And if you would say that my
lord has done you wrong, I am ready to defend him
from the charge without his bidding me so to do.
But the knowledge that I must die makes me bold
to speak out freely my will and my mind as I have
fashioned and moulded it.   Now, be that as it may
be, for if I die for my lord, I shall not die in dishonour.
Surely without a doubt is known the oath and promise
that you pledged to your brother, that after you Cligés,

who is going away into exile, should be emperor. And if it please God, he will yet be emperor. And you are to be blamed for this, for you ought not to have taken wife, but all the same you took one and wronged Cligés, and he has wronged you in nought. And if I am done to death by you and die for him unjustly, if he lives, he will avenge my death. Now do your utmost, for if I die, you will die too.

Beads of wrath break out on the emperor's brow when he has heard the words and the insult that John has uttered against him. "John," quoth he, "thou shalt have respite until what time thy lord be found, for base has he proved himself towards me, who held him right dear, nor thought to defraud him. But thou shalt be kept fast in prison. If thou knowest what has become of him, tell me straightway, I bid thee." "Tell you? And how should I commit so great a treason? Of a surety, I would not betray to you my lord, not though you were to rend my life out of my body, if I knew it. And besides this, so may God be my guard, I cannot say any more than you in what direction they have gone. But you are jealous without a cause. Too little do I fear your wrath not to tell you truly in the hearing of all how you are deceived, and yet I shall never be believed in this matter. By a potion that you drank, you were tricked and deceived the night that you celebrated your wedding. Never at any time, save when you slept and it happened to you in your dreams, did any joy come to you of her; but the night made you dream, and the dream pleased you as much as if it had happened in your waking hours that she held you in her arms; and no other boon came to you from her. Her heart clave so straitly to Cligés that for his sake she pretended to be dead; and he trusted me so much that he told me and placed her in my house, of which he is lord by right. You ought not to lay the blame on me for it; I should have merited to be burnt or hanged, if I had betrayed my lord and refused to do his will."

When the emperor heard tell of the potion which it delighted him to drink, and by which Thessala deceived him, then first he perceived that he had never had joy of his wife—well he knew it—unless it had happened to him in a dream, and that such joy was illusory. He says that, if he take not vengeance for the shame and the disgrace brought on him by the traitor who has carried off from him his wife, never again will he have joy in his life. " Now, quick ! " quoth he, " to Pavia, and from there to Germany, let neither castle, town, nor city be left where he be not sought. He who shall bring them both prisoners will

be more cherished by me than any other man.  Now,
set well to work and search both up and down and near
and far ! "   Then they start with great zeal, and they
have spent all the day in searching;  but Cligés had
such friends among them that, if they found the lovers,
they rather would lead them to a place of refuge than
bring them back.  Throughout a whole fortnight
with no small pains they have pursued them, but
Thessala, who is guiding them, leads them so safely
by art and by enchantment that they have no fear or
alarm for all the forces of the emperor.  In no town
or city do they lie, and yet they have whatsoever they
wish and desire, as good as or better than they are
wont to have, for Thessala seeks and procures and
brings for them whatsoever they wish, and no one
follows or pursues them, for all have abandoned the
quest.  But Cligés does not delay;  he goes to his
uncle, King Arthur.  He sought him till he found
him, and has made to him a complaint and an out-
cry against his uncle the emperor, who, in order to
disinherit him, had taken wife dishonourably, when
he should not have done so, seeing that he had pledged
his word to Cligés' father that never in his life would
he have a wife.  And the king says that with a navy
will he sail to Constantinople, and fill a thousand
ships with knights and three thousand with infantry,

such that nor city nor borough nor town nor castle,
however strong or high it be, will be able to endure
their onset. And Cligés has not forgotten to thank
the king then and there for the aid which he is
granting him. The king sends to seek and to summon
all the high barons of his land, and has ships and
boats, cutters and barques sought out and equipped.
With shields, with lances, with targes, and with
knightly armour he has a hundred ships filled and
laden. The king makes so great a preparation to
wage war that never had even Cæsar or Alexander
the like. He has caused to be summoned and
mustered all England and all Flanders, Normandy,
France, and Brittany, and all tribes, even as far as the
Spanish passes. Now were they about to put to sea
when messengers came from Greece, who stayed the
expedition and kept back the king and his men. With
the messengers who came was John, who was well
worthy to be believed, for he was witness and messenger
of nought that was not true and that he did not know
for certain. The messengers were high men of Greece,
who were seeking Cligés. They sought and asked for
him until they found him at the court of the king,
and they have said to him: " God save you, sire.
On the part of all the inhabitants of your empire,
Greece is yielded and Constantinople given to you,

because of the right that you have to it. Your uncle —as yet you know it not—is dead of the grief that he had because he could not find you. He had such grief that he lost his senses : never afterwards did he either eat or drink, and he died a madman. Fair sire, return now hence, for all your barons send for you. Greatly do they desire and ask for you, for they will to make you emperor." Many there were who were blithe at this message, but on the other hand there were many who would gladly have left their homes, and who would have been mightily pleased if the host had set out for Greece. But the expedition has fallen through altogether, for the king sends away his men, and the host disperses and returns home. But Cligés hastens and prepares himself, for his will is to return into Greece, no care has he to tarry longer. He has prepared himself, and has taken leave of the king and all his friends : he takes Fenice with him, and they depart and do not rest till they are in Greece, where men receive him with great joy, as they ought to do their lord, and give him his lady-love to wife ; they crown them both together. He has made his lady-love his wife, but he calls her lady-love and dame, nor does she for that cease to be cherished as his lady-love, and she cherishes him every whit as much as one ought to cherish one's lover.

And each day their love grew; never did he mistrust her nor chide her for aught. She was never kept in seclusion, as those who came after her later have been kept (for henceforth there was no emperor who was not afraid lest his wife might deceive him, when he heard tell how Fenice deceived Alis, first by the potion that he drank and then by the other treason). For which reason the empress, whoever she be, be she of never so splendid and high degree, is guarded in Constantinople; for the emperor trusts her not as long as he remembers Fenice.

Here ends the work of Chrétien.

THE END